Between Sea and Sahara

Eugène Fromentin

Between Sea and Sahara

AN ALGERIAN JOURNAL

Translated by Blake Robinson

With an Introduction by Valérie Orlando

OHIO UNIVERSITY PRESS

ATHENS

Ohio University Press, Athens, Ohio 45701
© 1999 by Blake Robinson
Introduction © 1999 by Valérie Orlando
Printed in the United States of America

Ohio University Press books are printed on acid-free paper ⊗ ™

03 02 01 00 99   5 4 3 2 1

Une année dans le Sahel by Eugène Fromentin
first published by Michel Lévy frères, Paris (1859) in the series
"La Bibliothèque moderne."
First English translation by Blake Robinson, 1999.

Library of Congress Cataloging-in-Publication Data

Fromentin, Eugène, 1820–1876.
    [Année dans le Sahel. English]
    Between sea and Sahara : an Algerian jounral / Eugène
Fromentin ; translated by Blake Robinson ; with an
introduction by Valérie Orlando.
        p.   cm.
    Includes bibliographic references.
    ISBN 0-8214-1272-8 (alk. paper)
    1. Algeria—Description and travel. 2. Sahara—
Description and travel. 3. Fromentin, Eugène, 1820–1876.
I. Robinson, Blake.
II. Title.
DT279.F93 1999
916.504'3—dc21   98-45880

Contents

Preface
History/Story

Fromentin is a man of contrasts if not conflicts. This devoted citizen of the Atlantic port, once redoubt, of La Rochelle is a lover of the land and culture of the Mediterranean. An avid frequenter of the Parisian salons, he is even more at home on a farm—he died of anthrax passed on by livestock. He clearly hates bloodshed yet thrills to military pomp. He is dismayed by the destruction of a heritage which he witnesses in Algeria yet is a proud, if sometimes reluctant, defender of what the French will call their overseas "civilizing mission." Finally, he is faithful to two mistresses: painting and literature.

It is not surprising, then, that this book is a blending of attitudes and approaches. Its mixed genre nature (travelogue cum essay, memoir plus fiction) is important. With hindsight, we can see the author readying himself for his masterpiece, the novel *Dominique*, to be published five years later. Of greater importance—certainly for the nonspecialist reader today—is the greater freedom fiction gives Fromentin to articulate what he has to say. In a sense, the epistolary device he employs is already fiction: there is no real correspondent, and the author is recreating events and places.[1] His decision to provide color, romance, and dramatic tension through recourse to fiction was made as the work was already in progress and in good part to make the work sell. One reason he had turned to writing was that his income from painting alone was so meager.

The first fictional character he presents is the mysterious, voluptuous Hawa. The painting by his hero Delacroix that enthralls him is *Femmes d'Alger dans leur appartement*. Hawa (borrowed from his "correspondent"/friend Armand Du Mesnil's unfinished tale, "Zorr") is, as he says, "the living form" of the central figure in the painting. Elsewhere he refers to an Arab man and his two sons as being a "living Bible." Fromentin naturally sees Algeria as landscapes, scenes, and even *tableaux vivants*. And, indeed, he manages his word pictures well. As Philippe Jullian notes, "Fromentin was more of a colorist with pen in hand than brush." But he also comments that, as concerns painting, "The Algerians of Fromentin are much more real Arabs than those of his artist colleagues."[2] Hawa, the coldly sensual—inhuman—beauty, is in part an erotic fantasy. She is literary kin to those Odalisques, who had already become a not uncommon subject in Western, specifically French, painting: the objectification of woman indeed.[3]

The other major fictional character, Vandell, is based on a real person who was well known in the nascent colony. He is very different from Fromentin's unnamed "correspondent." The presence of the latter, a brotherly friend and fellow "Algeria hand," in the background serves to reinforce the author's own ideas and views. In his "letters" Fromentin can say what he wants to him—and in his at times somewhat unpolished style—because he knows he will be understood. His real readers are reassured by the absent friend's receptive though fictional presence, identifying with him. "As you'll remember," Fromentin will occasionally throw in.

Vandell, however, who also becomes his traveling companion and friend, is very much present but hardly acquiescent. He is the protagonist, the other half of a Janus figure, his role that of the "scientist" to Fromentin's "artist."

The impetus to meld in his "journal" extraneous elements, including a tenuous romantic interest as well as opinions and data of a scientific nature, had several sources. The main one certainly came from within. Fromentin had an aversion to keeping the center of the stage, and he was proud, reticent, and self-doubting, aiming to create more than a travel book. While he did not wish to write a travelogue, he was even more averse to attempting a scientific compendium of things done and seen—the "document" approach he decried in painting. "Above all, it [nature] forced me to seek the truth beyond exactitude and a likeness beyond that of a certified copy. Absolutely rigorous exactitude is a very great virtue when imparting information, instructing, or providing a facsimile. It would, however, only constitute an asset of a secondary order in a work of this kind, providing there is perfect sincerity, a bit of imagination is mixed in, and time has been the one to choose the memories—in a word, an atom of art has been introduced."[4] Always seeking for that "truth beyond exactitude," the author wished to create a special way of telling things that takes up where painting leaves off, being careful that "his" (the author's) "pen didn't look too much like a brush sopping paint and that his palette didn't spatter his writing desk too often."[5] Furthermore, at mid-nineteenth century the social sciences, as we know them, including anthropology and sociology, existed only in embryo. Even archeology was at its beginnings, Fromentin still relying on the word *antiquaire* to designate a researcher in that field. George Sand, his friend and literary mentor, urged him to include both scientific information about geology and fictional elements to heighten the book's appeal. In other words, he was to conform more to current romantic fashion, which included a strong dose of "realism." She was delighted with the results, as was the French public.

While Fromentin is a *louis-philippard*, captivated by the "otherness," the light and color of this "Orient," Vandell is skeptical of the supremacy of French power and culture, taking the Algerians for both more and less than do most French, including Fromentin. He plainly tells the narrator that there is no point in his explaining to him what went on in former days at a given place because he, the narrator, is in no position to make sense of it: he doesn't know the people or its language—it's not his country. Even as concerns art, the efforts of Fromentin to give meaning to what he sees through his sketches is contrasted with the hundreds of drawings

Vandell makes, "like those of an architect." For Fromentin they are crude, hard to relate to. While the author's voice recounts what we might believe about this strange land in the throes of conquest and colonization, the book's hero, the loner Vandell, speaks with a different voice entirely.

Fiction has served its purpose in telling us about an important juncture in the life of a people, as well as that of its rapacious, conflicted, fantasizing master and one relatively enlightened artist. The image, the feel of a terribly resistant yet hobbled society that Fromentin presents us with is recognizable in the Algeria of today, rent by strife, wedded to grief. It is a bitter fact that its main locus —a place more or less of enchantment for Fromentin—is today called "the triangle of death," its apexes being specifically Blidah, Médéah, and Hadjout. Today's misfortunes are, of course, not unrelated to the country's past relations with Europe. Fromentin comments that the Ottomans had in the main let the country be; not so the French.

At the end of this history/story it is the leathery Arabist who "rides off into the sunset." The bourgeois Orientalist is going home to France to paint and to write about what he believes happens on the other side of the Mediterranean and in himself.

Notes

1. Fromentin made three trips to Algeria. The first was in 1846 for about six weeks; the second, the longest (September 24, 1847–May 23, 1848), was well short of the "year" of the book's French title *(Une année dans le Sahel)*; and the third was less than three months, providing the material for Fromentin's first book, *Un été au Sahara* and the excursion to El-Aghouat as well as much else in *Between Sea and Sahara*. He undoubtedly synthesized material from all three trips.

2. Philippe Jullian, *Les Orientalistes*(Fribourg: Office du Livre, 1977), 76, 122.

3. While antithetical to the canon of Fromentin the painter, the subject

was used by both Delacroix and Ingres (cf. the Louvre's *La Grande Odalisque* of 1814) and later, notably, by Renoir and Matisse.

4. Preface, dated June 1, 1874, to a new, third edition of *Un été dans le Sahara* (now *Un été au Sahara*). Eugène Fromentin, *Oeuvres complètes*, Gallimard (Bibliothèque de la Pléiade), 1984.

5. Ibid.

Introduction

L'Orient through the Traveler's Lens
Eugène Fromentin's Algeria

Valérie Orlando

Eugène Fromentin (1820–1876) was by profession a painter, best known for his "Oriental" subjects, yet he found himself seduced by the power of words. In addition to two Algerian travel books, Fromentin wrote *Dominique,* a psychological novel, which eventually became a classic although it is little studied today. His last literary contribution, *Maîtres d'autrefois (The Masters of Past Time),* written in 1876, offered a fascinating retrospective of Dutch and Flemish painting. *Between Sea and Sahara: An Algerian Journal* is the first English translation of Fromentin's travel book, *Une année dans le Sahel,* written in 1859. The translator's English title has been chosen to guide the reader, since today "Sahel," "shore" in Arabic, means the parched territory south of the Sahara, a strip of land between the desert and savanna. In Fromentin's era, the word designated this strip as the fertile band just back from the Mediterranean and well north of the Sahara.

The medium of the travel book offered Fromentin, author and painter, a means by which to meld the visual and the textual to form what he (and his mentor Théophile Gautier) called *transpositions d'art.* It was *par transposition* from one medium to another —the painterly to the literary—that Gautier explained would allow one to "recreate the beauties of the universe."[1] The world of "transpositions" was built on universalism, which upholds the idea that art is eternal and that painted depiction can bond with the written word as well as to music, sculpture, and poetry.[2] Despite being intrigued by this innovative theory, Fromentin believed that, although there is a certain artistic universalism for which an artist should strive, painting and literature are two art forms that inevitably express two different aesthetics. "It is without a doubt," he writes, "that fine art has its laws, its limits, its conditions of existence, what one would call, its domain."[3] Shifting from paint to ink for the artist was a way to extend real depiction one step further, "exactitude pushed to the limits."[4] His efforts to link the paintbrush to the pen aided the cause of *la littérature pittoresque* which Fromentin felt "took the art of painting and of writing out of their normal realms."[5] The author's new expression met somewhere in the middle of writing and painting by performing the new task of describing instead of simply telling.[6]

Fromentin's crisscrossing between, and subsequent amplification of, the worlds of artistic exposition[7] and journalistic expression created a new aesthetic, one that was not only artistic but a political reflection of the times in which he lived. This aesthetic became the popular body of literature and art known as "Orientalism," which grew into an entire scholarly, academic, and artistic discipline based on the exploration of the Eastern, primarily Muslim, parts of the world. "The Orient," as Edward Said notes in *Orientalism,* "was almost a European invention, and had been since antiquity a place of romance, exotic beings, haunting memories and landscapes, remarkable experiences. . . . [It became] an integral part of European *material* civilization and culture."[8]

Fromentin's quest to explain these Oriental symbols—this "new world"—was expressed in an innovative manner. Orientalism, as a literary school, was an artistic precursor of later endeavors by Symbolist authors, poets, and artists in Europe. While Fromentin claimed to be striving to present a neutral view of this conquered "other" and create a universal appreciation for a world that was so very unlike his own, both his artistic and literary efforts as well as those of other Orientalists of the time were directly responsible for influencing a lasting objectification of the "Orient." Victor Hugo's *Orientales*, written in 1829, comes to mind as an excellent example of the view held by French Orientalist authors of the time. Hugo writes, "The Orient . . . is a trampoline of liberty"[9] and thus provided a catapult, in particular for the French male author, to new planes of imagination evoking exotic, erotic, and sublime pleasure.

The objectification of the Orient insidiously assured France's continued love affair with ready-made stereotypes—Arabs as representatives of the exotic, the despotic, and the barbaric—that conveniently were associated with everything North African. The Orient would now and forever represent a place where one could lose himself, enraptured by and intoxicated with an idealized otherness, a comforting *lieu d'extase* (place of ecstasy) equal to the delight of a drugged euphoria—"to have done with life through a voluptuous suicide."[10] The Oriental euphoria traversed the Mediterranean and took root in the intellectual and artistic community of Paris. In the second half of the nineteenth century, *Turqueries* became the vogue in Parisian high society. Harem pants, satin slippers, and turbans were worn by intellectuals, poets, painters, and other popular figures of the time. *Keyf*, "fulfillment of sweet nothingness,"[11] became extremely popular as Europeans embraced what were viewed as Oriental perceptions of harmony and euphoria. Smoking opium and hashish was indulged in by men of literary notoriety such as Gérard de Nerval, Théophile Gautier, Charles Baudelaire, and Eugène Fromentin. In Paris, the Hôtel Pimpodan was a gathering place for the Club des Haschichins, whose members secretly partook in the pleasures of the pipe.[12]

This objectification and zeal for commodities from the Arab world amplified the representation of the Orient as a site of exotic bliss where the European man could realize all his fantasies. The alacrity derived from delving further into these new lands on a literary aesthetic level also greatly aided French political imperial policy. Imperialist rhetoric more and more found tools from the artistic and literary world to build on nostalgia for what once was, as well as a desire for what could be, a new era of international prowess for France.[13] The "commodification" of the Orient inspired exploration in Egypt, Turkey, and Indochina and laid the foundation for later Western sociocultural constructions of the other. These Oriental conceptions have remained as stereotypes in our century dividing East and West into familiar opposing poles.[14]

France's lust for the Orient, therefore, was built on a desire to create a great empire and a need to satiate a newly kindled hope to explore difference, recently brought to light by European adventures in newly colonized lands. Encouragement for this lust for the exotic was greatly aided by the mass media, which made it widely available to the public. Fromentin's and other Orientalists' ability to wield techniques like *transposition d'art* conveniently served the imperializing agenda, fueling the fire of exotica in both the art and literary worlds. In his travelogues, Fromentin cultivated his own arena of Oriental desire, as well as that of the public, by organizing his works in three categories. The first theme proposed the exploitation of stereotypes associated with North Africa; the second collectivized Oriental desire through explanation (to his reading public) for what Fromentin viewed as a mysteriously captivating space; third, the author transmitted the idea that travel in these new lands would lead the individual to self-knowledge and self-expansion. These three thematic areas reflected the political rhetoric of the 1830s and 1840s, echoing King Louis-Philippe's call for imperial development in the wake of declining revenues from older island colonies.

By 1828, *les vieilles colonies*, more popularly known as *les îles*—L'Ile Bourbon (La Réunion), Madégascar, and Haiti—were in decline or altogether lost because of economic and political circumstances in France and abroad. Latin America had proved to be a strong competitor in sugar and other agricultural goods, making French plantations unprofitable. The abdication of Emperor

Napoléon I on April 6, 1814, the subsequent restoration of the Bourbon dynasty, followed by the signing of the Treaty of Paris on May 30, 1814, by France and her allies, all called into question the practicality of continuing colonial missions. By 1815, France found itself faced with considerable losses as it was forced to cede its colonial economic world to Britain. The popularity of colonial ventures had waned considerably with the public since 1763 because it seemed that the slave trade created an artificial prosperity.[15] As early as the Revolution of 1789, the people of France had been divided over the question of slavery. Should postrevolutionary France promote colonialism when its people had fought to overthrow a despotic system and install a new ideology based on the rights of man, liberty and equality? Colonialism seemed too dependent on specificity and in a sense was being used to oppose the fundamental principles of the Revolution to subordinate people of color.[16] The divisions between those for and against colonialism became acute. It was clear that from 1828 onward the question of colonial missions would cause controversy for both the government and the people of France.

The *Affaire d'Alger,* which resulted in the military conquest of the city of Algiers in 1830, was born from a general malaise of the government in the wake of having to kowtow to British demands for imperialist concessions and the desire of the very unpopular Prince de Polignac, minister of foreign affairs, to reconstitute an empire based in North Africa. Using the breakdown of diplomatic policy with the Turkish dey of Algiers, Polignac persuaded the government of France to launch the Egyptian army led by Mehemet Ali against the three regencies of Algiers in an effort to establish French sovereignty over the western Mediterranean.[17] Yet Mehmet, finding good relations with the Turks and the English more to his advantage, scoffed at France's insistence on being the only European power in the region. The French military, therefore, acted on its own against the Regency of Algiers. On January 31, 1830, the king of France, against the wishes of the government, sent troops to the shores of Algeria, claiming that an expedition to Algiers would put an end to the pirates' reign over the Mediterranean and win back prestige for the French army, still recovering from its humiliating defeat,[18] and assure France's solid insertion into North Africa. The city of Algiers was seized. From 1830 forward France conquered more territory in Algeria. By 1847, Abdel-Kader, grand leader of the Algerian resistance, was defeated by the French army, shipped to France, and, contrary to the surrender agreement, promptly imprisoned. Only a few pockets of Algerian rebellion remained to be quelled. These were primarily in the Kabylia mountain region, the Sahara, and southern Algeria. Eventually, the army managed to subdue the rebel strongholds for the time being.[19]

Despite the strong and fruitful actions of the French military, approval of the conquest of Algeria was divided in political circles between those who condemned it and those who viewed it only as a means to conserve the tenuous throne of Louis-Philippe. Compounding the lack of unanimous government approval for the colonial endeavor was the general lack of support from the public.[20] A reticent public, however, was quickly swayed by the newly popular press in France with its reports from the colonies in the late 1830s and early 1840s. Thomas Bugeaud, organizer of the first large conquest in Algeria and later maréchal de France and governor of Algeria from 1840 to 1847, sent his imperialist accounts (describing the glory of war and conquest from the battlefield) directly to the burgeoning French journals of Paris, notably *Les débats*. He became well known for his descriptive, seductive, and captivating stories of the numerous bloody, "yet glorious," raids zealously carried out by the French army. The accounts of Bugeaud's military campaign and the earlier pieces by Théophile Gautier honed Fromentin's interest in North Africa. Both his Algerian travelogues, *Un été dans le Sahara* (A summer in the Sahara) and *Une année dans le Sahel* (*Between Sea and Sahara*), exhibit his ambition to be part of the politically expansionist climate of the times. In both books, the painter (now journalist) exploits the Orient on the imperial "accepted" political premise that the Arab world is utterly foreign and bizarre and is therefore in need of interpretation by the European. In each narrative Fromentin documents this "unknown" place for those who cannot travel there. He feels compelled to enlighten the public back home so that they may learn of this other world. Thus *Un été dans le Sahara* and *Une année dans le Sahel* are based on exploration and explanation, with the goal of bringing forth new ideals concerning alterity and difference. These ideals were essential in cultivating enthusiasm among the public for Fromentin's literary projects. Finally, this new wide-open space is seen as a place where one can better one-self through "manly" adventures against hostile elements of opposition, whether they be human or of nature.

Fromentin's travel companion and intrepid *adventurier*, Louis Vandell, in *Une année dans le Sahel* best exemplifies this image of a virile, "self-made man through masculine actions" that characterized the protagonists of many Orientalist works. Fromentin tells us he is "solitary," roaming the four corners of Algeria, a man devoted to adventure. He has gone completely native, adopting Arab dress and mannerisms. We are told that he has taken the Arab name Bou-Djâba, meaning "man with a shotgun" (the case for his telescope). "This country is mine, it has adopted me," the way-farer remarks. He has renounced any thought of ever going back to France, preferring to wander forever in the deserts of Algeria. "Vandell," Fromentin writes, "has been everywhere where one can go as an intrepid and inoffensive traveler, he has seen everything that merits being seen." The colonizing of Algeria thus has offered Vandell a platform on which to build an-other persona that allows him the freedom of exploration and a new identity. In addition to fashioning a new conception of himself, Vandell (to some extent reflecting Fromentin's own views) finds that the Orient offers a means to escape from French capitalist society, which, at this time, was in full expansion, leaving less and less space for dreamers, artists, and writers.

Traveling authors such as Gautier, Fromentin, Pierre Loti, and Gérard de Nerval, among others—they themselves mysterious as they wandered this Oriental world—also demonstrated the need to comprehend what they viewed as the unknown dark side of incomprehensible otherness. This space of alterity was a place of confrontation, or what Joseph Conrad would later call a "heart of darkness"—the colonized world that was both a site of curiosity and of repulsion for the colonizer. The Orientalist's expansion of his own "selfhood" by travel had a cathartic affect on readers and politicians. The fine line between literature and political rhetoric concerning the newly colonized lands demonstrates the influence authors like Fromentin had on the political climate. These authors gave back confidence to the public and assured them that this unknown world would not only lead to material wealth but also recreate the French man, thus fortifying the individual and, in turn, the nation.

The literary and artistic voyages by way of these ideals solidified the reading public's lust for knowledge of the new territories and assured Fromentin's personal quest for what he called the "complete aesthetic experience." This was an artistic undertaking that professed the goal of representing accurately—as a mirror—what really was *there*: "I look, but I hardly criticize. I concern myself with reflecting, in the material sense of the word; with inertia perhaps, but with the exactitude of a mirror."[21] In retrospect, however, rereading his texts a century and a half later, we cannot help but wonder just how accurately he depicted "reality." No matter how precisely he sought to portray Algeria and its inhabitants, and regardless of the sympathetic views of critics today who insist that the author-painter was misunderstood and did have a genuine interest in the welfare of the colonized, one cannot deny Fromentin's immense contribution to the cultivation of Western stereotypes of North Africa. Such constructions—convenient "typing" —had a lasting impact on the Maghreb for generations, placing the region, from this time forward, under a Western magnifying glass. As Said remarks, the Orient had been destined by the West to be "watched" because of its alignment with the bizarre, unknown, and mysterious. It became a place predisposed to drawing the attention of those such as Fromentin, "since its almost (but never quite) offensive behavior issues out of a reservoir of infinite peculiarity." It is the European, Said explains, "whose sensibility tours the Orient, [he] is a watcher, never involved, always detached, always ready for new examples of . . . [a] 'bizarre *jouissance.*'"[22]

Fromentin's Between Sea and Sahara: An Algerian Journal

After his second trip in 1848 to the fledgling French colony of Algeria, the artist dedicated his life to the pursuit of depicting the "Oriental" on canvas and paper. More than just representations, Fromentin's documents, both literary and artistic, aided in cultivating an understanding of and appreciation for the new colony among the French public.[23] Of particular importance is how Fromentin impressed upon the nineteenth-century reader that the "opening up" of the world through colonization places him (the author and the reader) in an optimally exciting position in which to explore it. As Vandell, his intrepid partner in *Between Sea and Sahara*, poignantly remarks when they take leave of each other, "There's my territory. . . . The world belongs to the man who travels."[24] On the heels of the military and with the words of the Orientalists' travelogues imprinted on their minds, settlers came to Algeria. Fromentin's "littérature d'ailleurs" created a new venue for artistic expression while assuring the everlasting melding of art and politics in the interstices between seduction and conquest.

Between Sea and Sahara is based on memories and notes of Fromentin from three different stays in Algeria. He organized and developed them as letters between himself and a friend in France in order to weave the story line of his texts. This friend, in reality, was his close confidant Armand Du Mesnil. Mesnil was sure that the author's collection of notes (documenting his year-long stay from November 1852 to October 1853) would be financially beneficial to Fromentin. Mesnil thus encouraged his friend to take advantage of the public's new love affair with the widely read serials in many newspapers and revues which had brought "high" art and literature to the common people. Before it was published in book form in 1857 by Michel Lévy, Fromentin's *Un été dans le Sahara* was critically acclaimed in its serialization in the *Revue de Paris* (June–December 1854). Subsequently, *Une année dans le Sahel* appeared in the *Revue des deux mondes* in 1858 before Michel Lévy published it as a book in March 1859.[25] The huge popularity of both books owed much to the form in which the texts first were presented to the public.

Rereading Fromentin in a Postmodern Context

Despite Fromentin's confidence that he was accurately portraying Algeria, "as a mirror," we must question the link between realistic depiction and the author's widespread public popularity. Like his paintings, which were often painted years after the images were sketched in a notebook, Fromentin rewrote much of the travelogues from notes more than a year after his return from Algeria in 1853.[26] Thus, after his work had undergone numerous revisions, embellishments, and input from friends such as Mesnil, one might speculate on the degree of "Algerian reality" Fromentin is really offering to the reader. It is, perhaps, for this very reason that we (students and scholars of Fromentin) need critically to review his, as well as other Orientalists', works to determine the accuracy of their sociocultural and historic depictions. Critically considering history and the West's depictions of the formerly colonized (as well as women, minorities, and others of the world diaspora of the disfranchised), leads us to the greater postmodern project: retelling history from all points of view.

This first English translation of Fromentin's work allows students and non-French-speaking scholars to consider links to other colonial authors of nineteenth-century Europe and America. By seeking to understand Fromentin and the era in which he was writing, we understand ourselves, as well as our foibles and the development of stereotypes and misconceptions we have about others. This is not to belittle Fromentin's contribution to the richness of French literature of the nineteenth century, but rather to attempt to place his writing in a historical context. His works are links that lead us to other realms of thought, as well as to an understanding of where codified modes of Western discourse concerning the non-Western other came from. Although he has been considered something of an enigma, Fromentin through his travels did launch an entire new body of dialogue between us and the other in the attempt to understand the "sum of human wisdom"[27] he so desired to bring to light in his works.

Notes

1. Théophile Gautier, *Voyage pittoresque en Algérie* (1845), ed. Madeleine Cottin (Geneva: Librairie Droz, 1973), 85.

2. Elmwood Hartman, *Three Nineteenth Century French Writer/Artists and the Maghreb* (Tübingen: Gunter Narr Verlag, 1994), 7.

3. Emanuel Mickel, *Eugène Fromentin* (Boston: Twayne, 1981), 44, citing Fromentin, *Un été dans le Sahara* (p. xiii).

4. Fromentin, *Un été dans le Sahara* (Paris: Georges Crès, 1924), 10. My translation.

5. Ibid., 6.

6. Ibid.

7. At an Orientalist exposition in 1847 Fromentin's first paintings *Une ferme aux environs de La Rochelle*, *Une mosquée près d'Alger*, and *Vue prise dans les gorges de la Chiffa* were well received, guaranteeing his public

popularity (Fouad Marcos, *Fromentin et l'Afrique* [Québec: Editions Cosmos, 1973], 35).

8. Edward Said, *Orientalism* (New York: Vintage, 1979), 1–2.

9. Jean-Pierre Lafouge, *Étude sur l'orientalisme d'Eugène Fromentin dans ses "récits algériennes"* (New York: Peter Lang, 1988), 13.

10. Fromentin, *Une année dans le Sahel* (Paris: Plon, 1884), 85 (p. 47 in the book).

11. Alev Croutier, *Harem: The World behind the Veil* (New York: Abbeville, 1989), 177.

12. Ibid.

13. So great was Louis-Philippe's desire to reconquer the lost prestige of France in the wake of concessions made to Britain in the early nineteenth century that he proceeded to "absorb Algeria into the French empire with little governmental planning, public knowledge, or actual support" (James Cooke, *New French Imperialism, 1880–1910* [Hamden, Conn.: Archon, 1973], 13).

14. As Edward Said and many contemporary cultural critics have noted, these first Orientalist depictions were responsible for affixing the labels of decadence, sexual licentiousness, corruption, nepotism, effeminate behavior, weakness, and childishness to the Arab world, most notably North Africa. See Said, *Orientalism*. The stereotypes born from the Orientalist depictions of the Arab world are being challenged and recontextualized by twentieth-century writers in French such as Assia Djebar, Leïla Sebbar, and Tahar Ben Jelloun. It is because of this link between the Orientalists and contemporary authors of the former colonial world that a "reopening" of the political Orientalist aesthetic of nineteenth-century France is interesting.

15. Jean Meyer, Jean Tarrade, Annie Rey-Goldzeiguer, and Jacques Thobie, *Histoire de la France coloniale: Des origines à 1914* (Paris: Armand Colin, 1991), 306–8.

16. Ibid., 313.

17. Ibid., 329.

18. Ibid., 330.

19. This, however, does not imply that the Algerian resistance was successfully eradicated. Throughout the next hundred years rebellion against the colonial regime would be constant. Isolated incidents of resistance finally culminated in the 1954 Algerian revolution, launching the bloody eight-year

Franco-Algerian war, which eventually ended with the defeat of the French and Algeria's independence in 1962.

20. Meyer et al., *Histoire de la France coloniale*, 335.

21. Hartman, *Three Nineteenth Century French Writer/Artists and the Maghreb*, 42.

22. Said, *Orientalism*, 103.

23. Hartman, *Three Nineteenth Century French Writer/Artists and the Maghreb*, 37.

24. Fromentin, *Une année*, p. 167 in the book.

25. Hartman, *Three Nineteenth Century French Writer/Artists and the Maghreb*, 37.

26. Mickel, *Eugène Fromentin*, 56.

27. Fromentin, *Une année*, p. 168 in the book. "Who knows? *Insha Allah*, if it pleases God! That's the final word—the sum of human wisdom" are Vandell's words to Fromentin on the latter's departure from Algeria.

Between Sea and Sahara

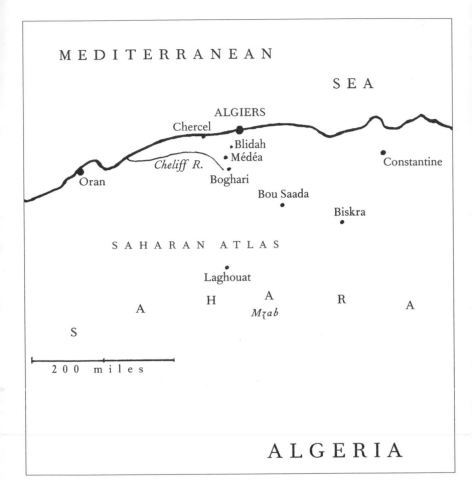

MEDITERRANEAN

SEA

ALGIERS

Chercel

•Blidah
•Médéa

Cheliff R.

Constantine

Boghari

Bou Saada

Oran

Biskra

SAHARAN ATLAS

Laghouat

A   H   A   R   A

S   A   Mẓab

200 miles

ALGERIA

1

Mustapha d'Alger

Mustapha d'Alger
October 27, 1852

As I WROTE YOU in my good-bye letter from Marseilles, I left
France two days ago and already I'm writing you from Africa. I
arrived today, October 27, borne by a strong northwest wind. It
was the only one Ulysses failed to imprison in his water skins, the
one to which Aeneas sacrificed a white ewe and the same one they
used to call Zephirus—a pretty name for a very nasty wind. Today
we call it the mistral. And so it goes, alas, with all the memories
left in these heroic parts by those Greek and Roman Odysseys.
The things themselves remain, but the myth making of travel has
vanished. Political geography has made three Spanish islands out
of the monster Geryon's[1] torsos. Speed has eliminated daring adventure; everything is simpler, more direct, not at all mythic, less
beguiling. Science has dethroned poetry. Man has replaced the jealous gods with his own strength, and haughtily but rather sadly we
travel in prose.

The Mediterranean is what it was. You can say all possible good
or evil about it but it's still the most beautiful, the bluest, and perhaps the most treacherous of all the world's seas. *"Mare soevum,"*
as Sallust said, no longer using metaphors, already talking like a

historian about the storm-racked waves that were bearing him to his African stewardship.

The passage over meant around forty-six hours of heavy rolling, too short a time to get you used to the sea, become fond of it, and take in the changing spectacle. Boredom compounded the discomfort of being in a bed rocked by some angry nursemaid. While inside it was like a hospital, outside there were grayish waves and a gray sky; the nights were long and dark and the two days wan in spite of the strong sun. The horizon was uncertain and the size of things distorted since the vantage point was so low—neither grandeur nor beauty. Islands retreated into the fog. Birds visited us en route, like island sentinels tasked with finding out who we were; others instead were thin-blooded emigrants fleeing from winter, going on ahead. There were still other birds, but in smaller numbers, who crossed our path heading north, navigating with unimaginable difficulty, almost touching the water. There were one or two sails on the horizon, wavering on those foamy hills. The wind in the sails made a great noise, the paddle wheels tore into the sea, and in the ship's bowels the piston worked with redoubled vigor. There you have the log of this short voyage, most certainly one of the least heroic ever undertaken over this fabled sea.

This very morning at nine o'clock, forty-two hours after having bid good-bye to the semi-African coast of Provence and three hours before entering the harbor we sighted land. The first thing of any height to be seen is old Mount Atlas; then the top of Bouzareah, which is nearer, appears; and finally Algiers, a whitish triangle set on a green plateau. Precisely at noon as the navy cannon were sounding, the ship's anchor was lowered. It was hot. The wind was no longer blowing; the sea was of a dark blue, the sky clear and deeply colored, and there was an odor of benjamin. I recognized this charming city by its odor. An hour later I was going along the road to Mustapha—chance had had me run into Slimen, my old coachman, at the entrance to the docks. He stopped in front of a small, square white house with a flat roof, and I was home.

And so the first leg has ended. I've come to Algiers being the closest to hand for that's the way I feel about migrations. I spent last summer in Provence, in a part of it that prepares you for this place, making you yearn for it: calm waters, an exquisite sky with almost the vibrant light of the Orient. It does not bother me to come to a place where my feet are on real Arab soil yet is only on the opposite shore of the sea that separates it from France and just across from the area that I've left. As I wait before moving on, I search for a title for this journal. Perhaps later on we'll call it *Travel Journal*. Let's be unassuming and call it for now quite simply *Journal of an Absent Man*.

This letter will not travel alone, my friend, for at this very instant I've sent you a messenger. It's a bird that I picked up at sea; I brought it along as a companion—the only one on board it felt good to get close to, and who kept his own counsel. Perhaps he'll forget that I saved him from drowning and remember only that he was my prisoner. He entered my cabin yesterday evening at nightfall through the porthole that I'd left open during a brief clearing in the weather. He was half-dead from fatigue and on his own he sought shelter in my hand as if so very afraid of the boundless sea lacking in reference points. I fed him as best I could. He didn't like bread at all, and so I spent the night hunting flies for him. It's a robin, perhaps the best known of all birds, the most humble, and with its frailty, its short flight range and homebody ways, the most interesting. Where then was he going at this time of year? He was going back to France—or was he perhaps coming from there? Doubtless, he had a destination as I have mine. Do you know— this I said to him before handing him over to the wind and the sea —do you know a white village in the pale-hued countryside along the coast where I might have glimpsed you, where bitter absinthe grows right up alongside fields of oat? Do you know a silent house that's often shut up, a road lined with lindens where people rarely walk, paths through sparse growth where the dead leaves pile up early in the season and where all kinds of birds make their fall and

Mustapha d'Alger

3

winter home? If you know that countryside, that country house which is my own, go back, if only for a day, and carry my news to those who've stayed behind. I put him on my windowsill and he hesitated. I helped him with my hand; all of a sudden he opened his wings. The evening breeze blowing off the land made up his mind to leave. I saw him shoot off in a straight line going north.

Good-bye, dear friend, for tonight. An absence begins whose length I don't wish yet to establish. But rest assured, I haven't come to the Land of the Lotus Eaters to eat of the fruit that makes one forget home.

Mustapha, November 5

To ALL those who think of me as a traveler, go ahead and let them believe that I'm traveling. Tell them that I've gone and if they ask you where, answer that I'm in Africa: it's a magic word that lends itself to suppositions and sets amateur explorers to dreaming. To you I can quite humbly tell things the way they are: I like this country, it's quite enough for me and for now I won't go any farther than Mustapha d'Alger, in other words a stone's throw from the beach where the ship deposited me.

I want to try to be *at home* on this bit of foreign soil where up to now I've only passed through, staying either in inns, caravansaries, or tents, sometimes changing lodging or camp site but always camping, coming and going with the freedom of movement of what's temporary, like a pilgrim. This time I've come to live, to settle down. By my lights that's the best way to see very little yet learn a lot. You see things by observing them frequently; you travel yet observe the show, allowing changing scenes to shift by themselves around a fixed point of view—an existence without motion. Perhaps I'll observe a whole year playing itself out and I'll learn how the seasons unfold in this blessed climate, reputedly changeless. I'll acquire habits that will become so many tight bonds wedding me to the innermost being of these haunts. I want to plant my memories as you would a tree, so as to remain, whether near or far, rooted in this adopted land.

What's the use of multiplying memories, accumulating facts, running in pursuit of oddities no one's written about or encumbering yourself with technical terms, itineraries, and lists? The exterior world is like a dictionary; it's a book that's full of repetitions and synonyms: a lot of equivalent words for the same idea. Ideas are simple, forms multiple; and it's up to us to choose and to sum up. As for famous places, I can compare them to rare locutions, a useless luxury that human speech can well do without, losing nothing. In days gone by, I did two hundred leagues in order to go live a month—that will live forever—in a nameless, virtually unknown date plantation; yet riding at a gallop I passed within two hours of the tomb of Syphax[2] yet did not waver from my route. Everything exists in everything. Why wouldn't the essence of the various parts of Algeria be contained in the small space that my window frames? Why can't I expect to see Algeria passing by under my very eyes along the high road or in the fields that border my garden? As I usually do, I trace a circle around my house, extending it to the point necessary for the entire world to be more or less contained within its boundaries, and then I withdraw within this universe. Everything converges in the center that I inhabit and the unexpected comes there seeking me out. Am I misguided? I don't think so, for this method, whether making sense or not, right off offers the greatest feeling of tranquillity and the promise of limitless leisure. It makes you look at things with a tranquil, more observant eye, that's, so to speak, acclimatized from the very first day. I'm living thirty-five minutes from Algiers, somewhat distant from town life yet all the same not lost among open fields. From here I can see the tower of the town hall atop a hill between two cypress trees.

The house I live in is charming. It's situated as if a lookout between the vineyards and the shore, commanding a marvelous view of the horizon: to the left Algiers and to the right the entire declivity of the bay all the way to Cape Matifou standing out as a gray-ish point between sky and water; and across from me is the open sea. I can thus take in a whole section of the Sahel and the entire Hamma: a long wooded terrace, dotted with Turkish-style houses that dips gently toward the bay and the narrow ribbon of the plains that connects it with the seaside. The countryside is one of boggy woods, but you also see meadows, orchards, cultivated fields, farms, and flat-roofed vacation houses with whitened walls, bar-racks that have been transformed into quarters for tenant farmers, old forts that have become villages. Everywhere there are roads, bunches of trees, and innumerable hedges of cactus and prickly pear looking just like silver embroidery. When the sun shines di-rectly on it you're able to see the somewhat whitish mass of Maison Carrée in the spot where the Sahel peters out as it approaches the delta of the Arrach. Nearer still to the cape you can see something twinkling almost on a level with the water: a little Maltese village that's called the village of the "Fort by the Water." In spite of the fever it thrives just a few feet from where Charles V's fleet went aground and his army perished. Beyond Maison Carrée you guess at there being an empty stretch of land where nothing moves, great spaces where the azure sky begins and the air is continually shimmering—the beginning of the Mitidja. Last, way in the back-ground, to the east, the ever-blue and jagged range of the moun-tains of Kabylia with their stern outline encloses this magnificent horizon that extends for some forty leagues.

At sunset Algiers is visible in profile at the other end of that semicircle, stretching in rows down the pitched levels of its steep hill. My dear friend, what a city! The Arabs call it *El-Bahadja,* the White City, and the name still fits even if since becoming French it's been dishonored. The lofty perimeter of its Turkish ramparts —scorched, dun-colored—has been broken through in numerous spots and already is no longer able to contain it. The upper city has lost its minarets and you can already make out some European-style roofs. All the nations of Europe and the world come dock their warships and merchantmen below the main mosque. Bordj-el-Fannar no longer intimidates anyone and as a sign of its tributary status flies the French flag. All the same, Algiers remains the capital, the true queen of the Maghreb. It still has its Kasbah, which it wears as a crown, with its cypress tree, the last vestige of the inner gardens of Hussein Dey.[3] It's a spindling cypress that points upward into the sky like a dark wire, yet from a distance it resembles the aigrette stuck in a turban. No matter what they do, it still is—and for a long time yet, I hope—El-Bahadja, that is, perhaps the whitest city in all the Orient. At sunrise when it lights up, tinged with a vermilion glow that every morning comes to it from Mecca, you'd think that only yesterday it rose out of an immense block of white, pink-veined marble.

The city is flanked by its two forts. While Bab-Azoun did not defend it, the Fort of the Emperor (Bordj-Moulaye-Hassan)[4] made possible its being taken. Farther ahead lie the outskirts, which happily aren't visible from here. The ships of the fleet with their fine architectural lines, heightened by intense colors, are reflected in a sparkling infinity in water of the tenderest blue.

The sun makes its way all around my quarters without ever entering. Inviolable shade reigns herein. Directly opposite me I've the unchanging northeast sky and the blue curtain of the high seas. The bluish semi-daylight that comes from the heavens spreads equally over the white walls, the ceiling, and the floor of flower-patterned tiles. Nothing is more sheltered yet more open, more resonant yet more quiet; in this redoubt, which is as conducive to rest as to work, there is a sort of cool, pallid tranquillity that's like a pattern of gentleness that deeply moves me.

I've almost two gardens. The first is small and is enclosed by walls. It's given to rose bushes, ficus, orange trees, as well as some tall, leafy trees that will lend me shade all winter long, and, if only in appreciation, whose names I'll learn as a result. To the rear I've a stable with horses; a whole company of white and blue pigeons are quartered above the watchdog's lair. One couldn't be more of a householder. Strictly speaking, my second garden is only a flower bed surrounded by a pasture made a bit green by the recent rains and which is coming to be scattered with wild mallow. A herd of cows (scrawnier than the beasts of Karel and Berghem)[5] go about all day long snipping the grass as fast as it grows and, where there are barren patches, licking the earth. These creatures bring to mind the poorer corners of France, and in my present frame of mind this memory is far from displeasing.

Once in a while two or three camels black from the scab, and followed by a little donkey, who with his long coat looks quite odd, encounter this herd of horned animals. The donkey lies down and goes to sleep. The large humped beasts spend long hours in dervish-like meditation. The shepherd is a young Arab dressed in white. He has a handsome face and his *chachia* shines from a distance among the cactus like a singular scarlet flower.

My bedroom faces south. From there I have a view of the hills that begin some fifty meters beyond my wall. The entire slope is carpeted with trees and colored a harsher green as the year comes to an end. Hardly visible are a few light-colored trees, old poplars turned gold by fall. You'd think they were covered with sequins. Only the almond trees have already lost their leaves.

The small houses are in the purest Arab style and have the whiteness of lilies: few windows, odd nooks, rooms that you can only guess at, circular divans indicated by small domes, and latticed openings that can set you to dreaming. The morning sky covers these mysteries with a cool, intense glow. The pigeons down in the yard coo, lending the proper musical touch to this pleasing picture. From time to time a pair of white pigeons trot along noisily on my windowsill, sending their shadows winging on to my bed.

Almost every day there are cavalry exercises in the hippodrome. The hippodrome is a vast empty space without greenery surrounded by olive trees and aloes, beginning where my flower garden ends and going up to the riverbank. You'll see Arab camel riders making a shortcut to avoid the main road to Algiers; Moor-

ish funeral processions on their way to Sid-Abd-el-Kader cemetery; as well as cavalry exercises from dawn to nine o'clock. Mus-
ket shots often awaken me. I hear galloping horses, the noise of
sabers clashing against stirrups, and the sound of trumpet-like
commands, clear and ringing. The riders maneuver in small squads,
walking, trotting, or sometimes charging at a gallop. Lines of
sharpshooters spread out along the edge of the field. The sun makes
the burnished copper bands of the cannons shine; you can see a
wisp of white smoke spewing from each weapon as it kicks back.
The acrid odor of powder even reaches my house. In the meantime, officers who are off duty proceed at a distance, working on
the agility of their pretty horses, so elegant with their narrow saddles, and delicately bridled as if with string. This is a daily spectacle. I don't like war, yet I feel myself thrilling at the smallest noise
that puts the idea in my head. The bugle's steady, virile sound, the
slight simulacrum of an engagement in the flashing of arms, the
movement of horses, is a moving thing, somehow marvelously at
home in the cheerful setting of an African morning.

Everything enchants me in this country at this time of year. The
stunning beauty of the sky would make even a graceless country
beautiful. Summer goes on even though we're in November. The
dampness of night refreshes the earth as it waits for rain, which
nothing leads us to expect. The year will close without sadness;
winter will come without our being aware of it, without dreading
it. Why doesn't human life end like an African autumn with tepid
breezes under a clear sky, without decrepitude or forebodings?

November 8

MY NEIGHBORHOOD is most peculiar. It lets you grasp just what
constitutes a colony in the process of creation. Of all the houses
that surround me, there aren't two that are alike and whose inhabitants are of the same group. All kinds of languages are spoken
within them just as there exist all variations of well-being and

penury. Activities are unfathomable, customs dubious, and lives mysterious.

Yet among all these bizarre households the strangest, there's no gainsaying, is a small house with a baleful aspect. Ramshackle and unspeakably filthy, it's situated a few steps from my own. It's inhabited by a legion of fowl: chickens, pigeons, guinea hens, and even geese. That entire feathered family exits each morning from every window and door. The more agile hurl themselves from upstairs and fly. They all return to the shelter at day's end, and the last hen is back in its roost before sundown. Sometimes a man appears at the entrance to the structure. He whistles to attract the stray birds and makes a circle with his arm, throwing handfuls of grain over the meadow. Blue-eyed and blond-haired, he's kept his pink complexion in spite of the sun. He's dressed in rough cotton cloth and sports a brimless cap. He takes deep puffs on his German pipe. My servant, who knows only his Christian name, informs me that he's a Pole, who's lived for several years in that chicken coop. I see him coming back every day at the same hour in the company of men who aren't known in the neighborhood. They're badly dressed and speak in low voices. The sweet odor of Moorish tobacco is mixed with the potent aromas of the hovel. They never light a fire or a lamp; they smoke and they chat; and then after the evening has spent itself in subdued conversation, the sad house becomes still. It's only at night, from midnight till dawn, that you hear the roosters crowing from this meeting place of exiles. If this miserable place's guests have no other lodging in a foreign land, they're to be pitied; and yet I ask myself by what cruel coincidence all those birds are being taken care of by people who probably have not always supped.

Mustapha, November 10

IN ALGIERS there are two cities. The French one, or, better put, the European one, makes up the low-lying districts and today continues on without interruption up to the suburb of Agha. The Arab one hasn't trespassed the boundaries of the Turkish walls and is concentrated around the Kasbah, where *zouaves* have replaced janissaries.

Of the old surrounding walls the French administration made use of everything that suited it, everything that concerned naval operations or commanded the gates to the city, everything that was more or less horizontal, easy to tear asunder and of easy access. It took the Djenina and demolished it, and made the old palace of the pashas into the governor's mansion. It destroyed the old prison, repaired the forts, transformed the jetty, enlarged the port. It also created a little rue de Rivoli out of Bab-Azoun and Bab-el-Oued Streets and equipped them with Parisian imitations; it chose among the mosques, leaving some to the Koran and donating others to the Gospel. It kept under its eye and close to hand everything concerning civil and religious administration, the courts and the clerical hierarchy. In its desire to guarantee to all religious and civil freedom, it had the places of worship and the courts next to each other. A small detail gives an idea of the nature of its politics; it allowed Catholic priests to wear the long, manly beard worn by ulemas and rabbis. It cut in two, but only out of necessity, the stairs linking the lower and upper portions of the city; it kept the bazaars in the middle of the new commercial streets so as to throw together different trades and provide everyone with the example of one people working together. Squares were created as so many centers for the fusion of the two peoples: Bab-Azoun gate, where they used to hang decapitated bodies above the heads that once belonged to them, was destroyed; the ramparts were torn down; the soap market, which used to be the gathering place of all the beggars, became Theatre Square. There *is* a theater, and to build it our engineers made the enormous ramp of the slanting Turkish battlement into a terrace. Once the old boundaries had been exceeded, the works continued on the eastern side since the sea intervened to the west and north. Extensive suburbs connect

Algiers with the Botanical Gardens. Last, the New Gate (Bab-el-Djeddid), the very one through which the army entered in 1830, was moved some hundred meters farther on. Today it's called Isly Gate, and a statue of that general and agricultural specialist was set up there as the permanent symbol of the French victory and takeover.

So much for the French city. You might forget there is another one. Not being able to do away with the Algerians, we've left them with only just enough space to live in up on the belvedere of the old pirates. This city grows smaller of its own accord, still clinging to this useless palladium. Unconsoled, it looks out over the sea which it no longer controls.

Between those very distinct cities there are no other barriers after so many years than those subsisting between the two groups, that is, distrust and dislike, and that's enough to keep them apart. They are the closest of neighbors without, however, mixing or becoming brothers except through what's worse in both of them, the common humanity of their vices. Below, the Algerians are in our territory; up there we still think even now that we are in theirs. Here all the languages of Europe are spoken and there only the clannish one of the Orient. From one to the other, about halfway between the two cities, an international, barbaric language is used called *sabir*, which is in itself descriptive. It means "to understand." Do we understand each other? Will we ever? I don't think so. There are unworkable combinations in moral philosophy as in chemistry and all the politics of the ages won't convert the law of human enmity into that of love. Peace gives the appearance of having been made but at what price? Will it last? And what will it result in? That is a big question being debated in Algeria as elsewhere, everywhere that the Occident shares an inch of territory with the Orient and where the North unexpectedly competes face-to-face with the South, its eternal enemy. We'll never stop the sons of Jocasta from hating, fighting, and killing each other. They fought each other in their mother's womb, and the flames of their funeral pyre will go off in separate directions, antipathy surviving in their very ashes.

Basically, the Arabs—our neighbors, at least those who are on our side—ask for little. Unfortunately, that little, we are incapable of granting them. They ask for the integrity and tranquillity of some permanent place of their own, wherever and as small as it may be, whether in the city or in the countryside, even if required to pay rent as they've done for three centuries for both good and bad under the Turks, who weren't up to us as landowners. They didn't want to be bothered, jostled, or spied upon. They wanted to live as they saw fit, behave according to their whim, and do everything as their fathers did—own land without its being surveyed, build without the streets being aligned, travel without their activities being scrutinized, be born without being registered, grow up without being vaccinated, and die without formalities. They claim as indemnity for what civilization has taken away from them the right to be naked, to be poor, to go begging from door to door, to sleep out of doors, to shun markets, to leave fields unsown, to scorn the soil that's been taken away from them, and to flee land that couldn't protect them. Those who have something hide and hoard it; those who have nothing take refuge in their penury. Of all the rights that have been taken from them the one dearest to their hearts is that of being fatalistic, that along with the independence of their poverty.

I remember how one evening during a visit to Blidah I encountered near the Algiers gate an Arab who was preparing his bed for the night. He was old, wretched in the extreme, got up in rags that hardly covered his body, worn out as if after a long day of travel. He paced the rampart, striving not to be seen by the sentinels as he sought out some corner among the rocks where he might make his bed. As soon as he saw me, he raised himself up and asked me as a boon my permission for him to stay where he was. "You'd do better to go into town," I told him, "and go lodge at the Foundouk."

He looked at me without answering, took his staff that already lay on the ground, tied his pack to his waist and went off in ferocious silence. I called him back in vain; he refused any hospitality put at his disposition within the walls of our town, and my pity had made him flee.

The thing that these voluntary exiles detest in us—for they do detest us—is not our administration, which is fairer than that of the Turks, our system of justice, which is less venal, our religion, which tolerates their own; it's not our enterprise, which they could benefit from, or our businesses that offer the means to acquire things. Nor is it our law enforcement since they have a long experience with being submissive, never having been contrary to the use of force, and, like children, they are agreeable to obeying as long as they can disobey frequently. The thing they detest is living close to us, that is us ourselves: our ways, our traditions, our character, our specific genius. They are wary of even our good acts. Unable to exterminate us, they submit to us; unable to flee us, they avoid us. Their principle and maxim, their method is to hold their tongues, to disappear whenever possible, and to remove themselves from people's minds.

I'd forgotten the upper portion of the city, which I'm now getting to after this long digression. Rendered useless, it escaped the plans afoot to make it French and so was saved from demolition crews and architects. Old Algiers was not destroyed. Looking at things for their picturesqueness, the best thing that could be done was to respect this last monument to Arab architecture and the Arab way of life, the only such along with, perhaps, Constantine that survives in Algeria and, while not intact, is recognizable.

The old Bab-el-Djedid gate more or less demarcates visually the two cities. There's a small lonely square exactly in this spot, a kind of neutral territory where French kids fraternize with Moorish youngsters or those of the Jews. The latter are the most adjustable in matters of others' origins; they sell scrap metal and old nails. The Kasbah's streets as well as those that go down toward the sea begin or end here; in this spot circulate customs, trades, noises, plus all the smells of these two worlds.

To the right the precipitous streets head off in the direction of Europe—you remember those poor neighborhoods that are mean and noisy and of ill repute. There are those green shutters, ridiculous signs, and the unknown ways. The streets are suspect and filled with suspect houses, with wandering sailors, tradesmen without a trade, police officers on the lookout; those cosmopolitan noises— and such noises!—immigrants going on in their violent dialects, Jews arguing, women swearing, Spanish fruit vendors singing obscene songs as they accompany themselves on Bianca's[6] guitar. To sum up: you'll find here the ordinary, bastard customs, that parody our small provincial towns, along with the depravity of our big cities, wretchedness shown to disadvantage, indigence in the form of vice, and vice in the form of ugliness.

Right across from that nameless agglomeration you can see modestly revealed those peaceful neighborhoods from the old Algiers that lead upward along bizarre streets toward silence. The transition is so rapid and the change of location so complete that straightaway you note the best and finest aspects of the Arab people, the very things that contrast with the sad sampling of our present way of life. Those people have as their very own a unique privilege that in spite of everything can ennoble them: they avoid being ridiculous. They are poor without being impoverished; they can be sordid but not trivial. Their lack of cleanliness reaches the grandiose. The beggars are epic in aspect, bearing within them something of Lazarus and Job. The Arab character is somber and violent but is never stupid or gross. It's always picturesque—in the good sense of the term—and artistic with no other proof than the way they conduct themselves. They act naturally out of I know not what higher instinct, thus enhancing their faults, the energy caused by whatever deformities being shared by their petty side. Their passions, which resemble our own, stand out more, making them more interesting even when they are reprehensible. Their conduct is unbridled but has no element smacking of the inside of a cabaret. Their debauchery is at least kept from giving off any whiff of alcohol.

Another rare quality they have is knowing how to keep quiet, thus sparing themselves having to be witty. "Speech is silver, silence gold," is a maxim of theirs. They are dignified, sober in language, honest in their dealings with people, and utterly courageous in their devotion. They are wild, uncultured, and ignorant. They embrace the two extremes of the human mind, the childlike and the genial, being exceptionally fond of the marvelous. With their outward gifts, on the other hand, they are a perfect example of human beauty. For an exacting eye, that's no small thing.

They hold on to these attributes with invincible resistance or inertia. In Algiers you can get the measure of that unfaltering obstination. They had every imaginable reason to be brought in line in spite of themselves, worn down through association and wiped away. They've kept their customs, superstitions, dress, and just about all the baggage of that stubborn way of life anchored in a religion of the past.

We may be able to dispossess them completely, expelling them from their final refuge without getting them to give up the least bit of their self-possession. They'll be annihilated before they're forced to abdicate. They'll have vanished before joining with us.

In the meantime, surrounded on all sides, squeezed—I was going to say strangled—by voracious settlements, guardrooms, and barracks, which to them are actually of minimal concern, they are voluntarily cut off from what is really happening. They are refractory to all progress, even indifferent to the fate that is being decided for them. Nevertheless, they are as free as any people can be that's been disinherited, lacks businesses, hardly has any trades, subsists almost in virtue of its very immobility, and is in a state approaching ruination. We are unable to tell, however, if they have given up hope or are merely waiting. Whatever the true feelings that hide beneath the extreme impassivity of those several thousand individuals, who from now on live among us, disarmed, their very existence just tolerated, they still have left an unassailable means of defense. They are patient and Arab patience is an arm that has an extraordinary temper. As the case with their steel blades, the secret process is known only to them. There they are, as they have appeared from all time, down their dark streets, shying from the sun, keeping their houses shut up, slighting trade, and minimizing their needs. They surround themselves with privacy as protection against the crowd, arming themselves with silence against the encroachments of the importunate, a scourge as serious here as everywhere else.

The very way their city was built is the most significant of symbols; their "white city" shelters them almost the way their national costume, the burnoose, a coarse, uniform wrapper, clothes them. Streets look like passageways, dark and often covered over; houses have no windows and low doors. They have the shabbiest of shops, where merchandise is higgledy-piggledy as if the merchant were afraid to show it. Trades are almost innocent of tools, and there exist only laughable little businesses—wealth can be stored in the toe of a slipper. There are no gardens, no greenery, at most a moribund vine shoot or an ailing fig tree in the rubble at the crossroads. You can't see the mosques. The baths are frequented in mysterious fashion, being solid, confounding blocks of masonry, constructed like sepulchers where life is hidden away and gaiety fears to make itself heard. Such is the strange town where a people lives, or rather, expires—a people that never was as great as was believed yet which was busy, enterprising, and wealthy. I was accurate in saying "sepulchers." Arabs believe they are living in their white towns; they bury themselves, wrapped in enervating inaction, overwhelmed by that very silence that charms them, enveloped in feelings of reticence, dying of lassitude.

What we perceive of their life in public, that is, what I call by analogy their trade or business is telling. They are embroiderers; cobblers; sellers of lime; jewelers of sorts; seed vendors also selling spices and tobacco; fruit merchants who sell oranges, water-melons, artichokes, or bananas depending upon the season; vendors of dairy products; and above all barbers as well as owners of ovens and cafés. That incomplete enumeration at least gives a fairly exact measure of their needs, defining better than all the old saws the practical reasons for the exceptional tranquillity these people enjoy, and that's the sole thing of interest to me in this account.

As in all the Orient, private life is protected by impenetrable walls. Private houses as well as shops have the same unobstrusive, if neglected, appearance on the outside. Doors only open halfway and close upon themselves from their own weight. Everything about these singular structures is shadowy, abetting admirably the secretiveness of their owners. The windows are barred, and every sort of precaution is taken regarding both indiscretion from out-side and inquisitiveness from inside. Two great mysteries reside behind these taciturn enclosures with their heavy, iron-grated doors as massive as those of a citadel: riches and the women of the fam-ily. One knows almost nothing about either one. Money hardly circulates, and the women are abroad very little. Cash is rarely seen except as it passes from one Arab hand to another to be transformed into a small item of food or drink or into jewelry. Women only go out veiled, and their most usual destination is the public baths, a place of inviolable shelter. Gauzy muslin curtains that billow in the breeze from the street or a flowering plant kept in a faience pot with a bizarre shape are about all that you can glimpse of these gynaecea. Noises that issue from them aren't noises at all but whis-pers that you'd take for sighs. Sometimes it's a voice that speaks from out of a hidden opening or that descends from a terrace, seem-ing to flutter above the street like the voice of an invisible bird; or sometimes it's the crying of a child complaining in a strange tongue, and the babbling mixed with tears has no meaning at all to the ear of a foreigner. Or perhaps it's the sound of an instrument, the atonal sound of the *darboukas* that slowly keep the measure of a song that you don't hear, whose sole note gets repeated like the vague rhyme that seems to accompany the melody of a dream. Captivity thus consoles itself, dreaming of a freedom it has never had and cannot understand.

The Arabs have a proverb that goes, "When a woman has seen a guest she no longer has any use for her husband." Arabs have a book of wisdom for their own use and the sum total of the politics of married life is governed by that precept. Accordingly, it's well established that whether delightful, luxurious, or impoverished, an Arab house is a prison with a sturdy lock, as tightly shut as a strongbox. Its greedy master has the key and he keeps within all his secrets; no one knows and no one can say what he owns, how much or how many or what the value is.

Much more tolerant than the Arabs are the Jews and blacks, who allow their women to go out unveiled. Jewish women are beautiful and, unlike Moorish women, are seen everywhere. You see them around the fountains, in the entrances of houses, in front of shops, or gathered about the bakeries when the flat bread is taken from the oven. And they go off with their filled water jugs or bread board, dragging their bare feet in their heelless sandals, their elongated bodies tightly wrapped in a sheath of dark-colored silk, all of them wearing like so many widows a black band over their braided hair. Walking along with their faces to the wind, these women in clinging clothes, cheeks exposed, and their beautiful eyes looking straight ahead appear singularly out of place in a world universally veiled.

Tall and well put together, their carriage is languid. Their features are regular and perhaps even a bit lackluster; their arms are ruddy and well-rounded and quite clean while their heels are dirty. Those who admire their type—and they are numerous—have to excuse somewhat this weakness of Jews of the common sort and be happy that their lack of cleanliness shows only on the heel like the human frailty of Achilles. Unruly little girls, who are gotten up rather more sumptuously than carefully, accompany these slender-bodied matrons whom you could mistake for their older sisters.

The rosy complexion of these youngsters isn't spoiled by the action of the sun as is the case with the little Moorish children, and their cheeks flush easily. They have a thicket of red hair such as ordinarily goes with the coloring of faces like these where blood rushes close to the surface. These heads diffused with light and capped by a sort of flaming underbrush provide a spectacle that's hard to imagine, particularly when the sun sets them afire.

Black women for their part, just like black men, are beings apart. They stride the streets briskly, with assurance; they never falter beneath their loads and walk along with the aplomb characteristic of a people who have an easy manner, fluid motions, and hearts impervious to sadness. They have a well-developed bosom, a long waist, and enormous hips: nature destined them for their double function of nursing their children and being beasts of burden. "Daytime a donkey, nighttime a woman," as a local proverb has it, that could be applied as well as to Arab women as to black. Their carriage, which includes a sort of shifting about that's hard to describe, helps throw in relief the robust opulence of their shape, as do their *haiks* bordered in white and fluttering like bridal veils about their large immodest bodies.

The Arab city affords more or less the customs and practices both public and private of yesterday. It's more or less the Algiers of the Turks, only shrunken, impoverished, having only the facsimile of a social fabric. Straightaway when you enter that city, going inside it as I do through a breech halfway along one side without passing through the European quarter, you forget history in the midst of the incongruities of the present and the ruins. Taking into account only what survives, you can still garner illusions to last a few hours, and such illusions are enough for me. If there were only one Arab left, you would still be able to retrieve the physical and spiritual character of the people; and if there were only one street left in the city (in its own right quite special for the Orient), you would with some effort be able to reconstitute the

Algiers of Omar and Hussein Dey. Political Algiers is harder to put together again for its a Turkish phantom that disappeared with the Turks and whose existence, no matter how real, seemed improbable even when they were here.

I made my usual, almost daily visit to the old section of Algiers. Generally, I don't concern myself with either history or archaeology. I go there in all innocence as if to the theater; it doesn't matter if the play is out of fashion as long as it interests me, striking me as new. In any case, I'm not difficult at all as far as novelty is concerned. The things I haven't seen with my own eyes are for me unknown. If I'm rather childlike in discussing them—as if going on about a discovery—it's that concerning art, whether right or wrong, I consider there's no need to be afraid of repeating anything. Everything is old, everything is new. Things change with the point of view. Only the rules of beauty are definitive and absolute. Happily for us, art exhausts nothing. It transforms everything it touches, adding to things even more than it takes away. It renews rather than exhausts the unremitting flow of ideas. The day a work of art appears, even if achieved as each artist will claim, with the purpose of following his own idea and the certainty of repeating no one else's work, that work will be done yet again. That's very encouraging for the intellectual life of humankind. So it goes with our problems concerning art as with all things. How many truths as old as the world will, if God doesn't come to our aid, still remain to be defined in a thousand years!

Now for today's walk. To begin with, I left my house, which you hardly know, and followed a road, which you don't know well, in a hired carriage, which is the practice in these parts. It would be ill-advised to spurn such a means of transport, which of course is less handy than going on foot, yet is far speedier and much more jolly, particularly when you travel with other people. The hackney used in Algiers is a carriage of open-work construction, built expressly for the south. It shields you a little like a parasol, the curtains, which are always in motion, fanning you. These carts, today quite numerous, particularly outside of town where I live, have as little suspension as possible and go horribly fast. Unbelievably, they never turn over. They're small omnibuses with a wide chassis sitting on skinny wheels, drawn by small Berber nags. These beasts, which are narrow chested and wheezy, have the slimness, sharp profile, and speediness of swallows. The vehicles are called *corricolos*. There was never a more accurate name for they go at a gallop, dashing through beds of dust, flying along like some mythological chariot down the middle of a cloud, offering their characteristic sky-borne noise of bells, slamming windows, and lashing whip. Whether the coachman is Provençal, Spanish, or Moor the speed is the same; the only thing that varies is how it's achieved. The Provençal man spurs on his team with curses; the Spaniard rains whip lashes; and the Moor terrifies it with a frightful noise from deep down in his throat. Whether well-paying or not, this occupation, so full of life, no doubt guarantees happiness for the carriage drivers.

It was Slimen in person who drove me in his hackney painted light yellow and called "The Gazelle." Slimen's a young Moor who's becoming Europeanized. He speaks French, baldly looks strangers straight in the eye, and stops at bars to drink wine. He was freshly shaven, fit and happy, and all gotten up in the colors of the rainbow—white trousers, pearl-gray jacket, pink scarf—and like a woman at a ball, wearing a pomegranate flower behind an ear. Managing his team with one hand, he smoked a cigarette with the other and every time he opened his mouth to exhort his beasts sweet-smelling puffs of air departed his lips. The neighbor on my right was a dignified old Moor who was returning from his plot with a harvest of onions and oranges in a straw container. Splattered with lime, a black mason sat across from me. He rocked with the bumping of the wheels, smiling at the joyous thoughts that occurred to him for whatever cause. To the rear there were three Moorish women with vanishing faces who babbled away beneath their white masks; they smelled of musk and pastries, and their *haiks* billowed out of the windows like delicate flags.

The conveyance was as I've described and the weather beautifully sunny, the morning air entering from all sides. As if drunk from the sensation of speed, I could well have believed that I was being led toward the liveliest, most joyous city on earth. The road is shadeless and everything close by it is powdered with white. Its shoulders were dotted with aloes that no longer have shape or color and olive trees paler than willows; what's far away disappears in a horizon drowned in mist and various hues of white. Wherever something moves along that long expanse of dust, looking ever more indeterminate after six months of drought, you see clouds of dust billow. If the slightest breeze passes over the countryside, the weighed-down tops of the older trees appear to dissolve in smoke. We follow the seacoast part of the way; farther on there's the suburb of Agha, lined with restaurants, bars, and inns starting from the exercise field all the way to Algiers, as if meant to scandalize the sober city where only water is drunk. It's a sacrilegious avenue whose main obeisance is to the grape. After that are vacant lots where battalions of donkey drivers bivouac. They come from many different tribes and not from among the richest. Finally, we come to a desolate spot, burnt up by the sun, stony even in the rainy season, and the equivalent in both color and state of abandon to a vast hearth in which only ashes remain. In the background there's a small fountain constructed in white masonry while near the road, no matter what the weather, shabbily dressed black women selling bread squat in a row on a rise; they wait for the improbable good luck of a donkey driver wanting to eat. To the right the old Turkish fort that today serves as a military penitentiary rises from a thicket of aloes, that resembles bundles of broken swords, its armed embrasures facing the sea. Drawing near, here and there we glimpse the sea. Its pale azure is glorious, moiréed with broad streaks of mother-of-pearl. Horses are being bathed, their tails out straight, heads high, their thick manes combed out like a woman's hair. They go in up to their bellies, then rear under their grooms. The sails of Maltese fishing boats silhouette their white triangles on the horizon like upright, scissoring wings of seagulls making a catch.

A little farther along on the outskirts another community begins: modern Algiers with a straight main street, six-storied buildings —a bit like an extension of the rue des Batignolles. One palm tree —you know it—hangs on. It's still there. Its base is cemented over, dishonoring it and yet not preventing it from dying. The broad fan of the tree has no new green growth. Black smoke whirls about its fruitless top; the cold rain of the hard winters has curled its spiky leafage. It resembles the people who planted it. It's cheerless yet carries on and may survive them. The traffic increases, leading you to expect a city. Here's the Office of Arab Affairs, which is an old Turkish structure, all white and *very* picturesque. Around it men on horseback, messengers with pouches across their chests walking with staffs and spahis in their red uniforms come and go. Across the street there's a butcher shop; skinny beasts are lined up beside it, their horns tied to rings in the wall. The door is open, allowing you to hear their death throes. The slaughterers have a ferocious look; knife clenched between their teeth, they seize the panting sheep and dispatch them, with Medea-like blows. These men are Mzabites, their part of the desert providing the best sheep and the best butchers. They are very black without being negroid and their dark skin is dyed violet by the abattoir's red flow—you'd think they were daubed with the dregs of wine rather than blood.

Here the road is almost impossible to describe, so encumbered that you find it hard to take in just what's going by. There are people on foot, on horseback, hay ricks belonging to the army, unescorted wagons bearing munitions, and beggars crowding the sidewalks. If you see a quiet bunch of people, they're Arabs; boisterous, and they're Europeans. Here and there, a camel rears up frightened by the tumult. Lines of women are heading toward the sea and legions of children of every origin take pleasure, here as elsewhere, in moving about among the bustling throngs. Smack in the middle of this crossroads, passing incessantly without being dispersed, are herds of little donkeys used to haul sand. Some of them are coming back to town with their baskets filled, while others, baskets empty, are trotting to the sand pit. The men leading the donkeys for the most part are from Biskri and wear a felt skull-cap, loose jacket, and leather apron or a laborer's overalls. These Biskris, who have their own customs, are a group of people worth getting to know and you find them everywhere. The donkey men too have their own cry that comes from deep down in the throat, strange and penetrating, imitating the call of wild beasts and calculated to frighten and so speed up the docile, steady pace of their convoys. Once loaded, the donkeys follow along, jogging when they trot. On the way back the drivers have no pity, mounting their beasts who are about as big as large sheep. They sit right over the croup with their staff resting in a break in the donkey's hide, a wound they continue to make worse and therefore more sensitive. They're very proud and erect as if manipulating prize horses. They hug the painful flanks of the donkey with their too long legs. They only have to extend a foot grazing the ground or lift it up so as to be alternatively walking or riding. They enjoy themselves in crushing with their bulk these small brave creatures. At the slightest cry, the slightest signal, the whole bunch spurts ahead in a straight line, ears flattened, with the hurried, sharp noise of a herd of sheep on the run.

At last you can see, though unclearly through a cloud of dust that is aflame with the direct rays of the morning sun, the entrance to Algiers, still called Bab-Azoun in memory of the long torn-down gate. Once you're there you have only to step down, settle the price of your seat (five cents in French money), and make your way up to the old Bab-el-Djeddid. In a few minutes you've made a long trip, immediately aware that you're two hundred leagues from Europe.

It was just about ten o'clock this morning when I reached my usual destination. The sun was climbing and the shadows were retreating imperceptively down the streets. The darkness massed under vaulted ceilings. The somber depths of shops, the black pavement awaiting noon and still resting in the softness of nighttime caused light to explode everywhere the sun struck. Above the corridor—like alleys—glued, so to speak, at the blinding angle of the balconies the sky stretched out like a dark, unblemished violet curtain that was nearly opaque. An exquisite time of day. The craftsmen worked as Moors will work, peacefully seated before their shops. The Mzabites in their striped *gandouras* dozed, sheltered by their veils; those who had nothing to do, and their number is always great, were smoking by the entrance of cafés. You could hear lovely sounds: the voices of children droning away in the public schools, nightingales in cages singing as if it were a May morning, and fountains gurgling within their sounding confines. I progressed slowly through this labyrinth, going from one deadend to another, by preference stopping in certain spots where a kind of silence reigns that was more unsettling than elsewhere. Please forgive me once and for all for the term "silence" that keeps returning in these letters more often that I should like. Unfortunately, in our language there's only one word to express all imaginable gradations of the very complex phenomenon that's utterly specific as to softness, weakness, or the total absence of noise.

Between eleven o'clock and noon, which is the hour when I'm almost certain I'll find my friends gathered together—I'm speaking of my Algerian friends—I was coming to the crossroads of Sid-Mohammed-el-Schériff. That's a place that I introduced you to the last time you were here, and it's there, my friend, that I want to take you again.

November 11

Do you remember the crossroads of Sid-Mohammed-el-Shériff? We'd spent what I call an "Arab morning" there. Do you remember the clothes merchant, a sort of rag seller cum auctioneer who sold a whole variety of secondhand goods, filling the street with his display? Alone, he was laden with the wardrobe of twenty women, with burnooses, brocaded jackets in addition to rugs. His shoulders and arms bore *sarouels,* leaf-patterned damasks, corsets with metal stays, belts shot with gold thread, and satin handkerchiefs. His hands held a profusion of earrings, bangles for the legs, bracelets; rings sparkled from bony fingers bent back like hooks, which when full resembled jewel boxes. Lost under that mountain of frippery, only his face unencumbered, his wide-open mouth fairly shouted the price of the first object put on the block. He came and went, going up and down the street between two rows of clients, never stopping and only infrequently closing a deal.

The crossroads is situated just about in the center of the original city, a short distance from the Kasbah. This is the last preserve of Arab life—the very heart of old Algiers. I know of no spot for conversation that's more out of the way, cooler—more suitable. One part of the crossroads has been done away with, the one facing south, so that you have right at hand, as lively counterbalance to the shade, a quite vast empty stretch filled with sun and with a view of the sea. The charm of Arab life is invariably made up of these two contrasts: a dark nest surrounded by light, an enclosed space from where there's an expanding view. The place is narrow affording the pleasure of breathing sea air while looking off into the distance. Making this abode more livable, and no longer dependent on the rest of the world, there's a mosque, barbershops, and cafés, the three most needed things for a people that's keen for news, has spare time, and is religious. Some folk pass through, some stop. Many never leave this place day or night, having no other bedroom than this public dormitory and no other bed than the platform in front of a merchant's stall or the hard pavement itself. Actually, that's where I encounter a great many of the city's unemployed; I've perhaps adapted myself to their example.

You know where we'd have our coffee; it was near the end of the street next to the shop of a Syrian. At the top of the street (it's on an incline) there's a school. Where the crossroads meets a seed store, to the right and left, just about everywhere, there are platforms spread with mats where men smoke, drink, and play checkers. The low door of Mohammed-el-Schériff mosque and the fountain for ablutions is directly across from us. In the midst of all that a sort of murmur rises from a crowd of milling people, neither noise or silence. The only real and continuous noise that you heard at all times was the voice of the merchant and public crier repeating his eternal sums: *tleta douro, arba douro, khamsa douro*, (three *douros*, four *douros*, five *douros*). Things haven't changed; you should easily be able to picture yourself once again in the midst of this small world.

The schoolhouse is still there. It will be there as long as the schoolmaster's alive and will be there undoubtedly after him—and why not? If you think like an Arab, there's really no reason for what has been to no longer exist since the permanence of custom comes to an end only with the end of things, their ruin and destruction through time. For us, to live means to change; for the Arabs, to exist is to endure. If that were the only difference between the two peoples, it would be enough to keep us from understanding one another. The schoolmaster is two years older than when you saw him; as for the children, the oldest have left and younger ones have taken their place. That's the totality of the changes: the natural evolution of age, of the years—nothing more. The schoolchildren continue to sit in three rows. The first is seated on the ground, the other two are disposed one above the other against the wall on not terribly sturdy platforms, set up with no greater care than shelving in a shop. It *is* a shop in the way it's organized and by the noise and glee emanating from its inhabitants. You'd think it were an aviary. The don, always in the center, administers, teaches, oversees. In three to five scholastic years he teaches three things: the Koran, a little penmanship, and discipline. He follows the book's verses, his hand resting on a long rod, flexible as a whip, that permits him to keep order in the four corners of the classroom without budging.

The café, and here I'm talking about the one that was ours and has remained mine, has as proprietor, as in the old days, that pale and handsome man, who's as serious as a judge with his white scarves and black cotton gown. All day long he's seated next to the entrance, smoking more than any of his clients; his elbow rests on the green box that's slotted like a bank that receives the day's take penny by penny. You're waited on by two little boys. One is a seven- or eight-year-old who's puny and very skinny; he makes a face since he sees out of only one eye. When he's not working, that is, busy bringing cups and offering the tongs holding an ember, you'll find him quietly seated at his boss's feet on a stool that's too high for him, forcing him to draw up his legs like a monkey. His name is Abd-el-Kader,[7] which is a very grand and difficult name to bear—like that of Caesar—and which seems ironical inflicted on a sickly constitution never to result in a man. The other one is the gentle, elegant type of Moorish child. His long blue gown that is his usual work attire hangs in folds as a dress would; in our world where the sexes are more clearly differentiated, he could pass for a pretty girl.

Such is the locus of my activities, and I could easily call it my "circle." I'm known and I know just about all the faces. As is due an habitué, I have my own reserved spot on the platform, as everybody knows. The company is very heterogeneous with people of every class and condition: I get language lessons as well as lessons in living. Concerning the Algerian friends I've mentioned, and who for the most part are acquaintances from the crossroads, I'd like you to know what fate has arranged for some of them during my absence. I'm afraid that some are no longer. Barring further information, I must think my old friend who was an embroiderer is among those individuals who have departed.

The oldest friend, both by age and the number of years I'd known him, was called Si-Brahim-el-Tounsi from his Tunisian origins. He was a Moor from a good family, an embroiderer by trade, who lived like a patriarch, but without his children, in a secluded shop. Our first meeting, which, alas, dates from a time several years distant, has already taken on for me the charm of memories from another age. I therefore mention this to you out of a double sense of loss. The man is probably dead today. It was the very night I debarked, in the middle of the night. I'd gotten lost in this section up from the port, which was even less well lit than it is today, in other words absolutely dark except when the moon was out. Everything was shut up, silent, dark. The only thing guiding me down the deserted street was the faint glow coming from a still open shop where there sat a sallow old man with white hands, his head wrapped about in muslin. A lamp threw light on his nighttime labors. Before him in a long-necked vase was a small pure white flower with the shape of a lily to cheer his lonely watch.

Having heard me approaching, he greeted me. He offered me his pipe and with a wave of his hand indicated that I should take a seat. With the serenity of someone who is at peace both with the world and his conscience he continued his work. It was eleven o'clock. The city was asleep. From down in the port I could hear the sea as it rose regularly, serenely—like the chest of a breathing human being. And this ever so simple yet complete picture struck me as having such virile melancholy and perfect harmony as to be a memory not to be forgotten.

When I got up to say good-bye, the embroiderer took his flower and, wiping off the stem, gave it to me. It's a flower that I don't know and have never seen again. I'm uncertain as to how to say or write its name and so hesitate to put down anything, but I understood it to be *miskrômi*. As such, whether made-up or real, the name appealed to me and I've never even thought to check to see whether it appears in any Arabic glossary. Sid-Brahim's shop is now occupied by a turner who makes ivory mouthpieces for pipes there where I'd seen the *miskrômi*.

On the other hand, Si-Hadj-Abdallah is alive—very much alive —and still in the same picturesque neighborhood, still in the rear of his shop that's stocked like a bazaar. Since he's perhaps a little thinner, the skin covering his cheeks is a little too ample; yet he's amiable, courteous, gotten out with the care of the well-born, and full of a happy man's good fellowship, still pounding his black pepper in an English bomb shard. This historical relic dating from Lord Exmouth's[8] bombardment, recalls a memorable date in the life of this sly old man, who's a perfect example of the Algerian shopkeeping class.

As for Naman, he's smoking hashish even more than ever. Because of this killing habit he's become even more bemused and takes less and less part in life. His pallor is frightening, and once you know that his sole nourishment is smoke, his thinness doesn't surprise. I can easily see him passing away, or if he hangs on until my departure, I'll certainly be saying good-bye for all eternity. He'll go gently from this world to the next in the midst of a dream that no agony, I hope, comes to shatter. Sleep is all he possesses of life when he does sleep, if he sleeps, which is probably not the case. Already he belongs to death given the unchanging repose of his spirit and his soul's lightness, its earthly ties three-quarters undone. This wise man then has solved the problem of dying without ceasing to live, or rather, of continuing to live without dying.

He recognized me, taking me perhaps for one of the regulars in his dreams for he didn't appear surprised, smiling at me with the ordinary smile given someone you've just seen the day before. He did, however, ask where I was coming from, and I answered him,

"From France."

"So you like traveling?"

"Very much."

"So do I. You learn through living," he added, "but traveling is better."

Stretched out on the same bench in the back of the café where I'd left him, he was smoking the same little pipe with the narrow stem embellished with a silver casing. He's lost all facial hair, his face being like that of a dying child. Some smokers judge the distance they have to travel by the time it takes to smoke a cigar. Right now you can calculate the number of pipefuls Naman is from Sid Abd-el-Kader cemetery. I'll be seeing him there.

November 15

THIS IS WHAT happened yesterday when I went to visit Sid-Abdallah. I note this incident as an aside, having no real merit and being outside the usual framework of my intellectual concerns. It's about meeting an Arab woman and is a peculiarly simple tale for it's made up solely of a musical impression.

Sid-Abdallah was showing me his family papers. He had extracted them from a little painted chest with a copper lock holding an antique watch and some valuable jewelry. They were sheets of parchment covered with the most beautiful script, enhanced with large waxen seals and blue and gold arabesques. Our friend told me about his background, that has him coming from a family of holy men. He had already talked to me about his noble lineage, but this was the first time he gave me official proof. Did he thus intend to increase his importance and make himself more worthy of my respect? Did he mean to acquire deference? That was already assured by virtue of his age and by what I knew of his person as well as the utter dignity of his manner. To me these things were far superior evidence than the certification of some parchments. It bothered me to think this might be a gesture of middle-class vanity coming from a person that up till then had seemed to me exempt of pettiness. All the same, nothing is haphazard in the way Arabs act, and once you know their ways, a confidence becomes, no matter what, an exceptional fact that can always make you ponder.

They'd just announced the one o'clock prayer from the balcony of the nearby mosque's minaret. Women were coming down from the upper sections of town to go to the baths. There was a crowd of them followed by black women carrying on their heads a fresh change of clothes. A lone woman without a servant or child suddenly stopped in front of the shop and leaned inside. Her greeting was the usual *salaam,* said with a soft voice, somewhat muffled by the muslin mask covering her face. Abdallah saw her but did not look at her; he had heard her greeting, answering it with a gruff *salaam,* and continued to go through the pieces of parchment without lifting his head.

"*Ouach entra?*" (How are you?), the voice continued more robustly but still somewhat cooing.

"Fine," Abdallah said brusquely, as if saying, "Be off with you!"

One or two rapid questions, however, finally made him stop reading; he reached out to the chest, slowly stacked the precious sheets, and then looked up directly at the woman. His blank face imperceptibly flushed and for the first time I saw his eyes, where shadows always lurked, show signs of life.

A very lively conversation was struck up, even if most of the time it was carried on very softly. There was no way I could follow the sense as words went back and forth. I was only able to distinguish the name Amar that was often repeated, and every gesture Abdallah made seemed to indicate refusal. Sometimes he held his beard in his two hands and defiantly shook his head, at other times he extended the back of his right hand under his chin and brought it up again in that emphatic way that accompanies the Arabic *la, la!* (no!). Without becoming discouraged, the woman instead kept up her attack, multiplying her entreaties, urging, pressuring, threatening, all with a volubility in phrasemaking, a manipulation of tone that would have made her impassioned harangue irresistible for any but old Abdallah.

The thing that I admired most in that very curious duel between grace and self-control, the pathetic and the calculating, was the charm of that woman's entreating voice—so clear and keen, so unfailingly musical. Whatever she was saying, she softened the harshest gutturals, and whether it was willed or not, her most forceful shows of emotion were wrapped in melody. That unrivaled voice never let a false note get by even when interjecting something or when rising with intonations of ire. I listened as you would listen to a virtuoso; at the start I was surprised and then delighted, not tiring at all as I listened to this rare instrument. Was it the song of a bird? How old was the woman and who was she? Unless it was a miracle of nature, there was some art—much art—in her way of talking. I guessed that she was over twenty. I'd seen nothing of her person, completely covered from head to toe as she was. She was enveloped in white and revealed only the edge of a delicate wrist that was tattooed with blue signs and adorned with twin gold bangles. Her pale, slender hands indicated a woman of leisure who was careful of her person.

The discussion ended without any resolution. The Moorish woman chose from the goods on display a sachet of *sbed* and a pair of embroidered slippers, whose sized she measured by placing one of them alongside her foot. She put it all in her *haik* without asking the price and then, adjusting her veils, bid good-bye to Sid-Abdallah with a nod of her head. Without thinking too much about it, I bowed, saying "Good day" in Arabic. "Good-bye," she answered in excellent French. At that moment I noticed her eyes directed toward me. I have no idea what they expressed, but I know that that look was most intense—I saw it take leave and reach me like a flash.

"Do you know that woman," I asked Sid-Abdallah after she had left us.

He had regained his composure; he calmly answered, "No."

"Do you know where in Algiers she lives?"

"I don't know."

"But what was she asking you for?"

It was too direct a question. The old man hesitated, then, as frequently happens in such cases, answered with a proverb, "Rather a pumpkin than a head without guile." At the same time he got up, put on his slippers, and left me, as was his custom, to go say his prayers at the mosque.

I'm familiar enough with Abdallah, or rather I think I am, to know that any reference in the future would have the double disadvantage of annoying him and not providing me with an answer. I decided that the best thing was to keep completely quiet. All I could do was note in my journal that perhaps for the first time in my life I had heard a wonderful female voice, a rarity in any country.

November 16

I WENT BACK to see Abdallah today. I got there a little ahead of schedule, having the firm intention of remaining discreet no matter what happened. And yet wasn't there already something like an admission of curiosity as I arranged that meeting for the following day with all the care due an appointment?

We'd been chatting for no more than five minutes when a woman, followed by a black woman dressed in a red *haik* (which isn't the style in Algiers) appeared down the street. I saw her go into the shadow of the overhang and then stop to adjust her veil, thus allowing the servant to precede rather than follow her. Her gown was of an impeccable whiteness yet I was surprised to see that she wore neither pantaloons nor hose as is usual in the city. Two heavy gold anklets clasped her somewhat skinny ankles and her naked feet were visible in high-backed shoes of black morocco. She walked in, with two bangles on her legs knocking together as if to accentuate her gait by making it pleasing to the ear; she made no movement, her head held high and stiff by the folds of her head covering, her hands hidden under her white gown. I became aware, however, that her eyes, which in the Egyptian style were lined with kohl, had widened in order to see me from askance; the stirring of the muslin that covered her cheeks like a mold led me to understand that she was laughing.

It was indeed my Moorish woman from the day before. I was warned by some kind of vague premonition, more meaningful than her sideways glance and her smile. I have to allow that my first impetus was to follow her. It wasn't acted upon. For nothing in the world would I have wished to be untrue to myself in front of my old friend; such an act of imprudence would have caused me to lose his respect for all time. She turned the corner and I heard for a moment the noise of those metal rings. The discussion we'd begun started up again in the most natural way. At the same time, I noticed that Sid-Abdallah didn't leave me at prayer time. Instead, rather unusually it seemed to me, he lost himself in small talk.

I regard highly, albeit with some embarrassment, these days, that excellent man, who with his simple manners is obviously very astute. And so to avoid a third encounter that might compromise both of us, my host and myself, I'll change my visiting hours henceforth starting tomorrow.

Abdallah has never spoken to me about his household, his marriage, and that restricted world usually rather numerous and complicated (nuptials are celebrated young and result in ample progeny) that constitutes the Arab family. I've learned from him specifically about his public life, that is, his birth, the social situation of his ancestors, his one or two trips abroad, and finally his career as a merchant. All that can be told in a couple of words.

On his return from Mecca (he is a *haji*) he set up shop in that same establishment where he lives now, and which you know. That was around 1814, when he was twenty years old. He doesn't say whether he was married but twenty years is already rather late for a young man of good family, particularly when the young man has been to Mecca. At the beginning he was solely a seed merchant. Since then his business has grown and if he's set aside a small spot in his shop for the sale of seeds, it's probably as a reminder of his younger years. You know what a well-to-do and upright Moor from a good family means by being in business: very simply, it's to be the owner of the only place on a main street where men can gather during the daytime and where he himself can stay and not be at loose ends. He receives visits and without leaving his couch takes part in activities in the street, learns the news brought to him, and keeps abreast of what's current in the neighborhood. To use a concept that is stripped of meaning when applied to the Arab world, I'd say that he goes on living in society without ever leaving his own hearth. As for the shop, that's a side activity. Clients are people whom he obliges by providing articles they need. There's never any discussion of price with him. How much? This much. Take it or leave it. The only thing that can annoy a merchant is to be busy a few minutes too many with a matter that doesn't appeal to him. If he wasn't counting on it, why should he feel he's missing out on money that chance will bring in and chance will take away?

The real point of a business as so construed is to take care of leisure time that you don't know what to do with. "You see," Abdallah said one day when explaining to me all about the social underpinnings of business in the Orient, "leisure makes *kief* and bad habits possible. Isn't that the way it is in your country? Frequenting cafés isn't proper for a man of standing, even less so for old men, and barely excusable for a young man. Cafés along with inns are meant for travelers and they're easy to recognize. Excluding them, the men you see there can be assumed to be vagabonds or beggars. All habits are bad that can compromise a decent man in such a way and make people think things about him that aren't true. Working with your hands is still the best thing since it makes you serene and diligent of mind. I belong, however, to a family that's always handled prayer beads better than a needle." There's some good in his code of conduct, particularly when you yourself put it to the test. Finally, Sid-Abdallah doesn't smoke, drink coffee, and wears only cotton or silk clothes of the utmost plainness.

I can add what I've learned from others to the information about him that I gathered from our chats. Sid-Abdallah is well-off but not rich. As a young man he had three wives but with the years cut back on extravagance. His most recent wife, who's now his only one, is young and lives nearby. I know the house, but of course he's never shown it to me and most probably I'll never step foot inside. I forgot to tell you that the other day I saw a fine twelve-year-old boy in his shop whom he introduced as his son. With wonderfully graceful manners the child took my hand, brought it to his lips, and smiled. I thought he would address me in French, but to my great surprise I learned that they hadn't taught him one word of our language.

I'd stayed with Abdallah for more than two hours after the appearance of the Moorish woman. As I was taking my leave of him, my old friend looked at me in a strange way. He continued to hold my hand with an intimacy that was not usual with him. Weighing each word he said, "*Sidi*, I speak as someone who knows quite a lot of things. Watch out for the Kabyle woman."

What bothers me the most, my friend, is the true meaning of what he said, which is open to several interpretations. I'm not talking about acting in a foolish way—and the danger is real if Abdallah has thought to warn me. Is the woman herself a Kabyle or is this a derogatory term that's meant to categorize her? A strict religious observer and quite intolerant, Abdallah detests and scorns everything to do with Kabyles and Jews. He uses the two terms, *Kbail* and *Youdi*, like curse words. "*Kbail-ben-Kbail*" (a Kabyle born of a Kabyle). In my presence this is the only violent language he's ever indulged in. He lends it a note of incredible aversion, making it the equivalent of "dog, son of a dog." In other words, if that's what "Kabyle" means to him, I know what I should think about the kind of woman she is. If he's wrong, I can't consider it a crime if she happens to be born in the mountains (the Kabylia). That can explain—providing an excuse—why she had forgotten to put on stockings when she left home to go to the baths.

December

THE WEATHER is still beautiful. You'd never believe that the year is coming to an end. Living in the open air as I do, rising with the sun not to return before nightfall, taking part minute by minute in the ebb of this season of smiles, I'm hardly aware of one day following another. I'm not aware of dates either; nor do I even try to retrieve the awareness that I've lost of time's passage, thanks to its too infrequent markers. The impression of the present moment repeats so exactly memories of yesterday that I no longer distinguish between the two. There's a lasting feeling of well-being that we don't experience in France living subjected to the oscillations of its changeable weather. Night suspends but does not interrupt the feeling. I forget that my sensations are being renewed since each day they're reborn identical and are always so keen and alive. Here as elsewhere, how the sky looks invariably determines my outlook. Both for the past month, if I can put it this way, have been steady fair.

That's my life in a capsule. I produce little, not even sure I'm learning much. I watch and listen. I give myself up body and soul to the mercy of nature, which I love. It has always done as it wanted with me and can reward me by soothing any upset, which is mine alone and which nature itself has made me experience. I test those filaments in my brain that are most sensitive and fatigued, wanting to determine whether any are broken, whether the keyboard is still in tune. I'm happy to hear it still plays in key, concluding that my youth is not yet over. Thus several more weeks of grace are allowed for the indeterminate pleasure of feeling myself live. Few people could accommodate themselves to a similar style of life. I would never propose my walks in the country, for example, to professional travelers. The way I see things, the life I lead has nevertheless some quite serious aspects. Perhaps you would agree with me. In addition, what else is there to choose from without being inconsequential? And why get stirred up when everything is in a state of rest? Why throw oneself mindlessly into the novelties of the morrow when universal life runs so peacefully with a hardly detectable flow within our habits' accustomed banks?

It's usual, my friend, to speak ill of habits, no doubt because people start off with the wrong idea. I myself have never understood why it should be a matter of pride to shield them or worth a great effort to get rid of them. Why describe as slavery what is God's law? Why, in the final analysis, should we imagine we are much more in charge of having chosen our path for not having left behind any signs? We are fooled; we end up belittling ourselves. Without habits the days wouldn't hold together—memories could no longer be grasped, no more than beads without their string. We belittle ourselves since, fortunately, it's impossible to imagine a man without habits. A person who says he's without any is quite simply someone who has a short memory. He forgets what he's done, thought, and felt the day before. He's not kept a diary! Or he's an ingrate who dismisses the days he's been alive. Concluding that they don't constitute a treasure to be cared for, he abandons them to oblivion.

If you go along with me thus far, let's cherish our habits. They're none other than the conscience of our being, arrayed in time and space to our rear. Let's do like Tom Thumb, who scattered stones from the door of his house all the way to the forest. Let's mark our traces with habits, taking advantage of them to prolong our existence and use the strength of our recollections. We should strive to make our habits good ones. Let's shift our existence to the right and to the left, if fate so orders, so long as it basically remains the enduring identity of our own selves! This is the means to rediscover ourselves in everything, not losing on our journey the most useful, our most precious piece of baggage. I'm talking about the sense of what we are.

What a gentle land this is. It permits great repose without interruption. Not a cloud, no wind—as much as to say there's peace in the heavens. Your body is submerged in an atmosphere that nothing disturbs. The temperature isn't even noticed, being so steady. From six in the morning until six at night the sun crosses unperturbed an expanse without blemish with azure its only color. The sun goes down out of the clear sky. As it disappears it leaves behind a spot of vermilion like a rose petal to indicate its exit gate to the west. A bit of dampness gathers in the foothills that spreads a slight haze over the farther reaches of the horizon. This process effects a harmonious transition between light and shadow; shades of gray accustom the eye to nighttime. The stars shine above the countryside that's growing blotchy now and the land's vastness becomes indistinct. At first you can count them one by one; soon they light up the sky. Night asserts itself in step with the complete withdrawal of the sun and half shadows replace daylight. All the while the sea sleeps on as I've never seen it sleep before, a sleep that for a month nothing has disturbed. It stays limpidly flat, becalmed, ever so lightly stippled by an infrequent ship's passage. It has the dazzle, the stillness of a mirror.

While it's no longer summer, we're still far from winter. You see few insects and don't hear all the springtime buzzing. The wild mallow has no height and the grass gets back its green but doesn't grow tall. This great stillness is only proper of course for a season of rest. Autumn in the countryside is a period of empty fields and quiet. French peasants say that *time is listening,* an ingenuous metaphor that calls up some kind of vague meditation, intuiting an element of interiority in such a silence. We are aware that we're no longer in the year's young manhood. Something that has suffered is getting back on its feet; there's a time of rest after great stress. You could call it the serenity of convalescence after the fevered ravages of a long summer.

It's nine in the morning, and I'm in a charming spot. It's halfway up the hills in sight of the sea, a grandiose foil that the seascape needs so as not to lose much of its effect, its character and depth. It's an empty place even though it's surrounded by summer houses and orchards. Solitude is supreme as in all the countryside hereabouts. The only noise I hear is the water buckets rotated by the mill, pouring water into troughs, and the almost constant rumble of the *corricolos* on the road to Mustapha. Before me are two Turkish houses grouped together at different levels so as to make a pretty picture without any real style yet having a pleasant Oriental cast. I observe the obligatory concomitant of any Turkish house:

each is flanked by cypresses. The houses are a blinding white, delineated by fine shadows as if by an engraver's tool. The cypresses are neither green nor brown—you wouldn't be wrong calling them black. That extraordinary dash of vigor stands out dramatically against the brilliant sky, outlining with brutal precision their compact form, the fine veining of the twigs as well as the branches' singular candelabra pattern. Rolling wooded slopes descend toward the valley below. The supple, serried lines of the farthest reaches of the hills elegantly ring in this portion of an intimate landscape. All this is quite unknown. That is, I remember nothing in modern painting that reproduces the seductiveness, the predominance of light colors with the further naive simplicity of a dominant three—white, green, and blue. Add the aggressive brown of the laterized soil; make the tall trunk of a white poplar, which is spangled as if by a goldsmith, rise up like some tree in a dream; then return some balance to this somewhat off-center picture by means of the horizontal blue line of the sea. You'll have once and for all the formula for an Algerian landscape of what was called the *fhas* before we provided the name "city outskirts."

I'm in the shadow of a magnificent carob tree that's famous in the surrounding country. It's said to be three hundred years old. The diameter formed by its shadow measures almost forty feet. The tree won't grow any taller, but it adds girth and the network of new branches keeps thickening. The continuing vigorous flow of sap has made its crown an inextricable mesh of crowded, nubby, interwoven branch systems. Soon it will have more twigs than leaves. No birds inhabit this dark-colored, spiky, and austere dome; its very solidity makes it immobile—you'd take it for a tree made out of bronze. Just looking at it, you feel it's indestructible. From time to time a still green leaf, but whose stem is already brown at the end, falls to the ground; another takes its place and the covering of leaves remains intact. You know, by the way, that the carob lives at least as long as the olive tree. I've seen bigger ones but none that had grown so nicely nor whose longevity was as probable.

There's nothing here measuring time's passage. No ailing sun, no sad-looking fields, no falling leaves, no trees covered with funereal mold giving them a sad look as if about to die. We are able to forget that life does slacken in this enchanted Hersperides where the word "waning" is never mentioned. How happy we'd be, my friend, if the permanence of everything that I see could make us believe in a possible perpetuity of things and beings dear to us.

From where I am there's a cemetery a stone's throw away. It consecrates the remains of a famous marabout, Sid-Abdel-Kader, who has rested for the past two centuries within a small monument bearing his name. The pavement of the courtyard conceals several sepulchers whose location is indicated by marble grave markers much worn by the going and coming of the faithful. The inside of the tomb with its tall, narrow, green-painted doors is not visible from outside and the pilgrims slip inside so stealthily the doors close on their traces. I thought I saw some small lamps alight, but that's all. These tombs are miniature monuments with everything on a small scale—courtyards, buildings, and even the domes that resemble skullcaps. An old Moor along with his family watches over the spot, which is twice consecrated—by death and by the piety of visitors. There are children as well as women—wives or servants—who come and go in the enclosure, treading with indifference on the graves' inscriptions. The peels of oranges mixed with leavings from meals are scattered here and there on the tombs; pigeons coo on the narrow stairs leading to the shrines. If it weren't for my great respect for these grounds, I could in one leap easily get myself on to its terrace. Most of the time two cats grown fat and lazy are the only guardians; they sleep curled up in the shadow of the tombs. From time to time the watchman himself comes to inspect the condition of the walls. He banishes the slightest signs of dirt with a small broom, a brush, and a pot of whitewash. He acts more as if he were painting rather than daubing with whitewash, reveling in bringing back through his handiwork the immaculate whiteness, which for the Moors is the sole bit of luxury

Mustapha d'Alger

43

the exteriors of their dwellings wear. He takes extreme care as if the most delicate task were involved. He's a big man with something of a belly, who's always cleanly dressed, with a face that's filled with equanimity. The spryness of his advanced years is no doubt due to the happy leisure hours afforded by his employ. When he's aware of my presence, which doesn't happen often since he's so busy with his cleanup, we greet each other politely with a few ritual words. Up to now I know this old man, who is half gravedigger and half sacristan, only from his greeting, "Good morning, *sidi,* may God's peace be upon you, may your household prosper, and may the death of your fellows exhort you to live in righteousness!"

This bizarre monument, which is half country house and half tomb; this sort of family life in the midst of graves; these children who are born and grow up on top of human remains; this unlikely juxtaposition of life and death; and finally, those lovely birds, associated as symbols of the utmost graciousness, whose sweet song resembles the posthumous gathering together of the many hearts that have gone on, of so many feelings snuffed out forever: all that, my friend—and believe me, with no kind of poetry involved —is of the greatest interest to me, provoking reveries that you can comprehend.

The public cemetery is next to the mausoleum and communicates with the restricted area by means of a door. It bears the marabout's name but it's also called the cemetery of Bab-Azoun, to distinguish it from the western cemetery near Bab-el-Oued. It's small for serving one-half of what's a fairly sizable city. The narrow plot is constantly being dug up, that is, where actual tombs don't enforce respect of the dead's property. I gather they are little concerned with the nameless persons buried there, making way in whatever way they must for the new arrivals. The soil, which is rich with human matter, supports enormous plants: mallow, cactus, and monstrous aloe thrive in abandon. A donkey strolls peacefully in the richly fertilized pasture.

Even the most opulent Arab tombs are very simple. They all resemble each other, which, from a philosophical point of view, exhibits great taste. A tomb is a rectacular masonry block a little off the ground. It has at its two extremities either a roughly carved turban atop a little column reminding you rather a lot of a mushroom cap on its stem or a triangular piece of slate placed upright in the manner of a sundial. The slab of stone or marble is covered by Arabic inscriptions, including the name of the defunct person and some Koranic precept. Sometimes the slab is carved in the shape of a trough and filled with soil. In this case you see a little grass and some flowers, either planted or brought there as seeds by the wind. Sometimes they think to carve into the two extremities of the stone two small holes in the form of a cup or pocket where rain is trapped, serving as a reservoir. "In accordance with Moorish custom, they carve in the middle of the stone with a chisel a slight depression. Rainwater gathers in the bottom of this funerary cup and serves in this torrid climate to slacken the thirst of the bird of heaven."[9] I haven't seen any birds flying toward these dry tombs or drink from these emptied cups. I'm still forced to think of "the last Abencérage" almost every time I enter the cemetery of Sid-Abd-el-Kader.

And yet you'd be quite mistaken to believe that all is edifying here. A mixture of charming fictions and absurd realities, reticence and unseemliness, delicacy and brutality constitutes the genius of the Arab people, making it difficult to define with any finality. One definition won't suffice; nuance is necessary. You may admire it, then right away think you're mistaken. Contradictions are frequent in this people's makeup; and there is a great clash between his native genius, which is subtle, and his upbringing, which is of the crudest. By temperament Arabs have a winged nature—no other civilized people has gone so far it that direction. It's therefore possible without contradicting yourself to think the most disparate things about them depending on whether you examine their thoughts or observe their customs.

Mustapha d'Alger

There's one day a week (it has to be a Friday) when the women of Algiers, under the pretext of paying homage to the dead, gather in crowds at the cemeteries, a little like Constantinople, where they come together at the *Eaux-Douces*.

It's just a pleasurable get-together, an outing in the country, and for those who are married, and I've reason to believe they're the smallest number, that husbands consent to. Furthermore, these gatherings occur almost every day, and of an afternoon it's rare for the enclosure of Sid-Abd-el-Kader not to be enlivened to the greatest possible extent by chatter and laughter. They do more than talk. They eat, they install themselves on the tombs, they stretch out their *haiks* using them as tablecloths. A gravestone makes do as both seat and dining table, and in small groups they indulge in pastries and eggs with sugar and saffron. The long veils, which aren't needed when there are no peering eyes, are hung in the cactuses, where they flutter, leaving the colorful under layers of clothing visible. It's in part spectacle being the occasion for emptying chests so as to show off outfits. They cover themselves with jewelry, on the neck, arms, fingers, feet, bosom, waist, and head. They paint their eyebrows in the liveliest colors as well the area around the eyes and drench themselves with the most violent scents. Who knows what kind of tales they tell of neighborhood doings, gossip, domestic indiscretions, petty plots and intrigues. Freer here than at the baths, they have as confidants and witnesses the discreetest sorts, those who are under their orders at home. I take part in this spectacle fairly often, hidden in a shady observatory which I've chosen for this purpose. I see everything, hearing only a general muttering, a mixture of guttural or high-pitched sounds, a sort of chirping comparable to a big flock of gossipy birds. Their ranks thin out as dusk draws close. Omnibuses that are parked not far from the cemetery, like our hackneys outside public places, carry the worldly faithful off to Algiers by the carriage load. And it's only when night has fallen over them that the dead are at rest.

A little farther down the road from the cemetery there's a quite noted spot. It's often seen in pictures, and you must have seen at least a dozen—thus sparing me, I trust, from giving you mine. I'm talking about the "plane tree café." Assuredly, the site is pretty. The café with its dome and low galleries, well-proportioned arches, and squat columns is sheltered by immense plane trees of magnificent height, girth, and presence. Beyond them lies an Arab fountain, which is linked to the café by a very imaginative, long, curving wall of striped brick work with fretting near the top. You hear primitive spigots constantly running in the basin. It's all quite encrusted with age, a little worse for wear, and while baked by the sun has turned green from moisture. To sum up, a pleasing dash of color that makes you think of a Decamps.[10] A long line of low, broad steps faced with bricks laid flat and bordered with rounded stones follows the road's slight incline leading to the drinking trough. There you'll see trotting up herds of donkeys making music with their hooves, or caravans of camels that slowly clamber up to plunge their long bristly necks into the water in a way that, depending on what angle you're looking from, can either seem very ungainly or very beautiful. Across the way, through a French-style iron gate flanked by columns and fronted by sad acacias is the long entrance way to the Botanical Gardens, lined with roses already in bloom. I go there once in a while, but I won't say anything about it, not being a botanist, and in any case, studying only those things pertaining to Arab life.

evening of the same day

I ENDED the day looking from among the trees at the Turkish houses. There's a whole section of the hill where there are a great number of these elegant buildings. You see them quite close one to the other sticking out here and there from the greenery. They are all so well landscaped that each gives the impression of having its own park. Each is built in a picturesque location on a succession of wooded slopes with a sea view. If you yourself climb to the top of this vast amphitheater evenly divided up in terraces, you can imagine the fine, wide-angled view that the inhabitants of these pretty dwellings, these days belonging exclusively to Europeans, must have. The great mystery they enclosed is also gone along with much of their charm. The architecture of these houses hasn't much sense when applied to the customs of Europeans. You have to take them for the fineness of their exteriors, studying them like so many gracious monuments of an exiled civilization.

When they were lived in by the people who built them and I could say dreamed them, these dwellings were both the most poetic and the cleverest of creations. These people knew how to make prisons that were places of delight, cloistering their women in a porous, spacious seclusion. By day, they had a multitude of small openings in walls as well as gardens strung with jasmine and grapevines; by night, they had the terraces. What could be more spiteful and yet at the same time solicitous as concerns the distraction of the prisoners. These confining houses hardly have any fences to speak of; the countryside manages to intrude, taking them over. The tops of the trees reach their windows; by stretching an arm you can pick leaves and flowers. The odor of orange trees envelops them, perfuming the interiors.

The gardens resemble artistic playthings meant for the amusement of the Arab woman, that singular creature whose life, whether long or short, is never anything but a kind of childhood. Now you only see the sand-strewn pathways and small marble compartments in which sluices have been carved, from which water is made to meander in mobile arabesques. As far as the baths are concerned, they can only exist in the fancy of the jealous, poetry-loving husbands. Just imagine vast tanks in which the water is only a meter deep, lined with squares of the most beautiful white marble, and with arches that give on to an empty horizon. No tree reaches that high, and when you are seated in these aerial bathtubs you see only the sky and the sea and are seen only by the passing birds.

Our sort understand nothing of the mysteries of such an existence. Walking in the countryside we take delight in it but return to our houses and shut ourselves up once more. That confined life by an open window, the immobility before such vastness, the luxury existing on the inside, the mild climate, the slow passing of the hours, the habit of lethargy—before and around you, everywhere the same sky, the radiant countryside, the infinite seascape—all of that must produce strange reveries. Also, it must sap your vital strength, changing your nature; it must combine what we can only call the ineffable with the painful feeling that being a captive means. And so there were born in the depths of these delightful prisons a whole order of pleasures of the mind which we can hardly imagine. All the same, my friend, maybe I've gone astray in attributing rather literary reactions to creatures who assuredly would never have had such.

Mustapha, end of December

I SPENT last night listening to the dogs bark. The countryside was full of noises; I think that roundabout there wasn't one animal whether loose or tied up that wasn't giving tongue and that I couldn't hear. As the night was damp and still air being a good conductor, I calculated as the noises somewhat slackened that the faintest of them must have reached me from more than a league away.

At first I was fearful of a fire but detected no lights at all either on shore or out in the bay. Except for those yapping beasts all was profoundly, securely asleep under the peaceful gaze of the stars. The dogs were barking in reply to each other, as is their habit, for somewhere one of their kind must have lifted his voice first. The signal having been given to all the kennels, the alarm went out from neighbor to neighbor and on a calm night like this one, it wasn't impossible that the extended barking could reach the other side of the Sahel, from hut to hut, farm to farm, village to village, extending as one continuous echo all the way to the depths of the plain.

I got to sleep toward daybreak and yet—should I admit to such childishness?—that odd night seemed short to me.

I wouldn't be able to write down, not even having been able to make notes at the time, what I recapitulated in the way of recollections, the number of places I saw as well as the number of bygone years that I seemed to be reliving. They were rapid visions lasting a moment yet so full of life, going straight to my heart like a needle. They came one after the other as precipitously as noises, and what's really bizarre, in the middle of all that quite indistinguishable barking I was able to sort out quite different notes and particular tonalities, each one having in relation to my memory a precise significance and corresponding to reminiscences. Some represented certain provinces in France, others some period or some adventure in my life that I thought lost yet wasn't—above all, my life in the country and the years when I was traveling, the two periods when, becoming interested in the noises of the countryside, my way of life was at its most active. How many were the odd places in western France in the vicinity of the Channel or in the south! How many the small villages whose names I've not retained, and which that night I so to speak lived in for a few seconds! All this was due to the astounding apparatus of memory at work on sounds.

Other sounds that were fiercer or hoarser, and more like caterwauling, brought back to me my sojourns in Africa. I recognized them for the most part by hearing them being repeated at the same distance and from the same direction at constant intervals. I could listen anxiously for the sound that corresponded to such and such memory either to savor more fully the pleasure that I was experiencing or to make it return when others interrupted.

Almost all those "visions" have vanished this morning except for a few whose traces remain. Above all I remember having thought for a long while as I listened to the very familiar bark of a bedouin's dog: it was a bitter freezing night spent in a small *douar* at the far end of the *tell* of Constantine. I was deep in the mountains in the roughest of terrains far from any road where I'd arrived in the evening after a long ride. I'd had just a few minutes of daylight in which to ready a camp site, set up my tent in the center of the *douar*, and so be under its protection. All about, the terrain was mud, garbage, and debris; the frost returned at dusk and luckily made everything hard. In addition, the ground was littered with the carcasses of animals that had either been slaughtered or, more likely, died of starvation. The winter, which was severe, had killed off a good number and the suffering was terrible in the small *douars* of the *tell*.

The whole night the small sheep plus goats, which had been gathered within the enclosure and kept as close to possible to the tents, coughed, baaing in pain. The children, who were chilled to the bone and couldn't sleep, moaned within the households' miserable shelters; and the women groaned as they rocked them without being able to banish either the cold or their sleeplessness. The dogs bayed as they kept themselves moving within the *douar*. Upset by the light from my lantern, they circled about my tent. I'd tied it down carefully and hammered the pegs well into the ground. As soon as I put the light out, the circle they formed grew smaller, and up until morning I could hear them scratching the ground and sniffing as they stuck their muzzles underneath the skirts of the tent. I felt on my face their breath like that of wild beasts. That night was awful and I didn't shut an eye. At first light I left the *douar*, not to return.

This recollection is one of the thousand I could cite. It's short, that's why I've called it to your attention. The whole history of my life enfolded before me during those few hours of wakefulness. It was somewhat light in my room with its white walls, and that transparent partial light was my mysterious companion. Around five in the morning, the baying began to let up and I went to sleep.

Mustapha d'Alger

THE CHANGE in the date alerted me that we had gone from one year to the next. There isn't a day that isn't the occasion for some anniversary or can't be made the starting point of a new year. Even if the January date has been adopted because of an alignment of mores and habits, it's imprinted as well on what I'd call the predilections of our conscious state. It's a good idea to have a calendar about even when traveling. I suddenly remembered that time flies for everything and everybody, as well as for me. Instead of being cradled in obviousness as I had been these past few days, I felt I was being carried away by a swift current. I said to myself that it's never prudent to let the months float by without a reckoning: time flies by unawares, and you're unable to make out what it was used for. It's often a bad sign when you can say about a year, "My, how short it was!"

A calm life under an ever so caressing sky in a pleasant land. That something or other that resembles life for having taken over freedom and leisure, having retained none of the bonds or annoyances, hardships, worries, or the heeding of good examples, or duty almost. The abandonment of self combined with the abandonment of so many things. Does all that have its own logic?

In one's extreme youth there are whole years—long years—when the sole residue, alas, is contained in a miniature of a woman. And those are years without weight or substance. Ours, my friend, are of another dimension, having a different heft. They should leave behind them something better than the residue of ashes and scent.

One day at sundown I was in a village in the south here and the evening was so beautiful it was dangerous for a constitution by nature too susceptible to repose. It was on the edge of a pool beneath some date palms. Bathed by warm air, permeated with silence, under the sway of extraordinarily sweet perfidious sensations, I remarked to my fellow traveler, "Why should we move on to somewhere else, so far from such sunny well-being, so far from peacefulness, so far from what's beautiful, so far from wisdom?" My companion, who wasn't the kind to philosophize but simply a man used to an active life, answered, "Get yourself back in a hurry to a country where it's cold. You're in need of the north wind to spur you on. You'll find less sun, less well-being, above all much less peace, but you'll see men there, and whether you're wise or not, there you'll live, that's the way the law is. The Orient is a much too comfortable bed to lie in. You stretch out, feel at ease; you're never bored for you're already dozing. You believe you're thinking and you're sleeping. There are many who seem to be living who haven't existed for a long time. Look at the Arabs, look at the Europeans who make themselves over as Arabs in order to acquire the means—slow, convenient, wrongheaded—to have done with life through a voluptuous suicide."

I won't go back to those northern countries before the time I choose. All the same, I'll be assiduous in keeping in mind the advice that was given me. Since such is the primary defect of solitude, since such is—at least on me—the effect of silence, blue sky, and deserted pathways, from this day forth I'm returning to the land of the living.

Mustapha d'Alger, January

UNTIL NOW I've only given you a broad portrait of the Algerians. I talked about gravity, discretion, a natural dignity in their bearing, in their language and habits. I'd wanted to point out those general traits which strike you straightaway when you are fresh off the boat from a European country where precisely those qualities are among the rarest. Let's not forget, however, that there are two peoples here, who resemble each other when compared with us yet are absolutely different when analyzed separately. We've looked at their similarities; today let's look at their differences. Let's give back to each the heritage he jealously guards. And so let's leave the Arabs where they are in the countryside, settled in villages or wandering with their tents. Since I'm living now in Algiers, let's discuss the Moors. Perhaps their portrait will in actuality lose something by being truer to life. It might be that precision instead of enhancing their features will diminish them.

Algiers is an Arab city inhabited by Moors. Moors make up three-quarters of the indigenous population. The remainder are a mixture of blacks, Biskri, and Mzabite immigrants; Jews, who speak the common language and have stayed the same since their coming here under Titus and Hadrian; and finally some Arabs, but in such small number that you can say positively there aren't any Arabs in Algiers. Furthermore, that city was neither their capital nor citadel except in their imagination: it was the headquarters of a government they disliked and an administrative center which they disobeyed more often than not. They were fond of it for the honor of the Crescent but not at all out of any interest in the last of their pashas. They had never assimilated their cause to his; such was their indifference as regards this modern Carthage that they let it fall without giving a hand, without foreseeing that it was they themselves being undone as they abandoned it. They had invested in it only a small part of their pride, on deposit under Turkish protection, as the people of the Sahara do with their harvests in the silos of outsiders. Their true destiny lay elsewhere. They reserved the right to defend it on their own territory, man to man, and that long war in the interior, and which is just now coming to an end, showed the way they understood politics and the way they waged war.

Historians have written much about the Moors. Where do they come from? Who are they? To what Oriental grouping should they be assigned? Are they the aboriginal people of this country? Do they come from the Moors of Spain who were defeated and thrown back upon the shores of Barbary? Are they, as has been also said, the direct descendants of an invasion that preceded that of the Caliphs? Or should we see in them, on the contrary, the quite mixed result of all such invasions? Mightn't there be in the veins of this people with their charming but indeterminate features a composite of barbarian and Greco-Roman blood? You have there a small sample of the hypotheses. The question is nebulous; the ancestry of the Moors has yet to be decided.

Whatever the blood relationship between Arabs and Moors, and whether or not they were originally close together, today there's no way of confusing them, nor do they themselves wish to be confused. Perhaps if there aren't two races, there are two branches and two very distinct families which in reality have nothing in common except their language and religion. They don't resemble each other in physical type, customs, way of life, temperament, makeup, or dress. They don't like or respect each other; their interests are contrary. They would act on their enmity if our presence didn't create for them a certain amity amongst themselves, having now the common bond of antipathy for us—the brotherhood of rancor. One group are still feudal countryfolk. Travelers and soldiers, they are numerous and resourceful. They are in all respects a great people by their origins, history, and traditions. They are heroic in the style of Alexander the Great and as adventurous as he was. Like him they wage war as if it were a journey—but with arms. Parents to a religion that nearly covered the globe, they spread to the farthest extent of Asia without becoming the masters, properly speaking, in any place. They came to inhabit incomparable lands, their faces always wearing that air of nobility, which is the very beauty of their destiny. The other is a smaller group, typically of artisans, shopkeepers, rentiers and scribes, who are middle class and petty in their ways, tricked out in their dress. They're elegant, but without any grandeur, and good-looking rather than beautiful. Comfortable but no more so and never poor, they never attain splendor whether as a form of luxury or abject poverty. Both groups have their pride. To use the wrong name with either one is an equal affront to both, as with two persons related by blood.

What's most lacking with the latter group of people is precisely what the first possesses in excess, and that's something that I'd call grandeur or to talk like a painter, style. The Moors have no style at all. That's partly due to their person and partly, too, to the environment in which you see them. Everything around them is somehow diminished and serves to make them seem so: their narrow streets, their shops that are hardly fit to enter, their sedentary life, and their way of squatting Turkish fashion rather than reclining as the Arabs do. Their dress is elegant but has no drape. It's narrow, lacking in either bulk or folds; it adds nothing to a man's importance and in fact lowers the estimation of what you might suppose him to have. A gown that's more ample, for whatever reason, makes you presume stronger passions, more greatness of soul. It's a matter of *artistic* prejudice, if you want, but in this case, of course, I'm speaking as an artist. With their tightly fitting jackets, their Turkish trousers that look like skirts, and their belts that many of them let hang loose, it's as difficult for the old to appear majestic as it is for the young not to have an effeminate air.

"Effeminate," there now's the word I believe that suits for it defines their make-up. It also fits their tastes, defines precisely their aptitudes as well as summing them up both physically and spiritually—it passes judgment on them. Isn't it in the nature of countries with gynaecea to engender a sort of confusion of the sexes, weakening the one in the measure that the other is degraded? It's a strange thing that at the moment that she disappears from public life, woman becomes manifest in the general temperament of a people; the less importance accorded her on the outside the more accrues to her through the bloodlines. She is looked down upon because of the mistreatment shown her: she is cloistered, lazy, and made one with *objets de luxe* and playthings. Man, however, replaces her and comes to resemble her and the substitution degrades him. Woman gets her revenge by degenerating the species and the species is punished for a societal fault.

The result is what we observe: a whole people that's almost feminine—boys that are nearly girls, young men that you'd take for women. They are beardless, fine-featured if a little soft, somewhat rounded in shape, nothing strong and resolute; an uncertain beauty that's never manly right up to the age when youth itself is erased by the weightiness of the years. The opposite of the Arabs for whom indolence is the right of the male. With the Moors it's the husband who's industrious, and I mean that he uses needle and thread. He works with wool, dying, weaving, and sewing it. He not only makes his own clothes but those of the women and children, including their shoes and even his jewelry and theirs. His alone is the art of crocheting and embroidery; he knows how to marry colors, how to combine silk and gold thread. He possesses looms, skeins and balls of yarn, bobbins, heddles, scissors, a whole arsenal of instruments that look strange in his hands and make him pitiable in the eyes of those neighbors of his adept with swords. While he's lacking in strength, he did at least inherit its opposites: he has alertness, manual dexterity, delicacy and grace. He is intelligent, flexible, and docile; he can calculate and if business suits him only up to a certain point, he thinks highly of it rather than scorning it. As lackadaisical at his workbench as he is carefree in his shop, as little diligent at his sewing as he is unhurried about selling, he considers both commerce and the trades as pastimes. Work exists to round out his leisure rather than occupy his life, and to tell the truth it's a means of distraction, a relief from the boredom of resting.

The Moors don't like horses, hardly own any, and ride them badly. Their rather flimsy harness jars with the substantial one of Arab horses. You have to have a real horseman's kit and war gear to fill with dignity the high-backed saddle and plant your feet in the Turkish stirrups. They wear the black leather sandals of those who stroll but walk little and in winter they never wear boots, only knee-length stockings. Trailing spurs would make it impossible for them to walk. Evenings, you can run into some of them—those who are rich—as they head off toward their gardens on the back of a mule. They ride sidesaddle on wide, flat saddles that are quilted like a palanquin and lead their tranquil charges with flicks of a switch, never having recourse to bridle or heel. That's the sum total of their riding skills. Many old men wear glasses, something that's quite unknown among Arabs, being superfluous since their eyes seem never to fail them. These folk are the money changers, the scribes and schoolmasters, in a word the *tolbas*. They write with a reed on small squares of paper placed without any support in their left hand, their long, copper writing case sheathed in a fold of their belt, just below the heart where warriors carry a dagger. Writing case, reed pen, a few sheets of paper, plus an old manuscript of the Koran which few people read and a very small number understand: that's all there is here, by the way, to call to mind book learning, yet that is little enough to distinguish Moors from Arabs, who are even more unlettered. The great mass of the people, moreover, read little and don't write. They smoke, dream, watch and talk as they work with their hands. They spend the long days among the shadows, in the cool azure of the bazaars, which is where men of the same people are expected to pass their time outside their homes. The bazaar takes the place of a forum. It represents both workplace and public space, everyone is in everyone else's home and in his own.

In the bazaars you'll find cafés, scents, flowers, and birds. Nightingales sing within little cages made of porcupine quills hung from the overhang in front of shops. Beneath the cages and on benches you see young men seated next to each other with embroidery on their knees and a spool of gold or silk thread stuck behind an ear. They're clean, well got out, and their faces are a little lighter than pale amber; lightly attired, their necks, legs, and arms are uncovered; they have jackets of carefully chosen colors, belts that go from red to a bright pink and white pantaloons with myriad pleats that balloon around them when they're seated. Whether they're at rest or at work the pose is elegant and there's much languorousness in their eyes. To top off their not being men, they almost always have flowers brushing a cheek. The tobacco they smoke is fragrant and the voluptuaries among them smoke *tekrouri*, that is, the leaf of the Indian hemp plant ground to a powder, or to use the well-known term, hashish. That's what they call making *kief*. Strictly speaking, *kief* is a peaceful state of well-being carried to tipsiness, produced by any drink or inhaled drug. It indicates as well the sensation experienced when eating sherbet or smoking a pipe. It's improperly applied to the object itself; for instance, I've asked for *kief* and been understood by the *tekrouri* sellers.

A taste for hashish always goes with a love for birds. In Constantine certainly, but also in Algiers, every smoker of hashish owns a nightingale. Naman is the only one I know, who, because of poverty or obliviousness to the everyday things of life, doesn't have one. I don't know whether it's worth mentioning, but the very pragmatic nightingale is a hearty eater: the better he's fed, the stronger and more limpid his song. They give him finely chopped raw meat into which butter is kneaded. Such hardy fare perks up the bird, who catches his breath and starts to sing. The Lord only knows . . . maybe the contentment that comes with a full stomach. The tenderness of his mode, the rhythmic feeling and passionate soaring make you forget the bird, hearing only the musician. Who hasn't been enchanted and lulled by him ever since the species has existed, living among us either free or in prison? Isn't this the eloquent soul of tenderness, the very music of human sentiment? He seems to express what we all feel. A lover discovers in him his tender feelings, a person who's suffering, his bitterness, and a mother who's afflicted, her despair. "Bard of our nights of happiness!" said of him one of this century's most unfathomable dreamers. "Young Albano[11] cries out that already the beak of the nightingale has knocked on springtime's triumphal door." Wits dulled, the smoker listens in his own way to that wordless song, reaching him as it can through the thick layers of his dreams. Would he understand, my friend, if I told him that it had made a man named Obermann[12] cry because he was alone at the lake's edge, feeling that he was a grown man and weak—someone who hadn't lived?

The other day I attended a session of the cadi's court. I saw how justice is meted out. It would be hard to imagine more becoming procedures or ones better able to justify having a trial. It's all easy, intimate, and relaxed. The court is located on rue de la Marine in the courtyard of the mosque. The same door takes you to both tribunal and church, the same site serving both justice and religion. Thus the person to be tried as well as the judge are under the closest possible scrutiny of God. The courtyard is tiled and closed off at one end by balustrades facing the sea. A fountain and two small structures stand out among shrubs, rose bushes, and large evergreen banana plants in the center. The smaller of the buildings, which is not as busy, is the mufti's; he represents the court of appeals. The other one, which the French administration rebuilt a few years back in a style that's more or less Arab, is the court of first instance; the cadi occupies it. The overhang, which is very pronounced and Oriental looking, protects a wide landing up two steps, where participants leave their footgear and sit in the shade while waiting for their case. A large Dutch door allows the public to be present at the proceedings; at the same time it illuminates the hall, which has no other apertures. The small whitewashed hall is square, arranged and furnished in the simplest way. On either side a row of benches up against the wall behind a row of tables serve as desks for the clerks and assistants of the cadi. At the entrance there's a wooden stool for the process server (a *chaouch*); on the floor are mats where clients may squat. At the far end opposite the door is the cadi's place, what would in France be called the tribunal, that is a dais with a desk and a low couch backed in green stuff with some cushions. To the rear there are just a few false windows in the form of niches; some small closed armoires, the archives, holding a few books and papers; and finally, above the judge, an inscription in large letters from a verse of the Koran.

The function of the scribes *(adoul)* is to follow the questioning, examine the accusations, and establish the verdicts. You can recognize them by their singular headgear, a length of white cotton stuff made to look like a pumpkin, their silk cape entirely covering their pantaloons, as well as by their graver, more dignified air, which distinguishes them from the common of men, thus revealing that they are magistrates. Don't forget that the *adoul* are both men of the law and of the cloth, presiding over worship services and burials just as they oversee judicial disputes. Through this double ministry they can affect the most serious concerns of both present and future life.

As for the cadi, his responsibilities make of him an important figure, even in relation to our French jurisdiction. He is the most accomplished sort that I personally know among the upper middle class of Algiers. He's tall and thin with a black beard that's somewhat sparse; his eyes are gentle and wise; his bearing is very distinguished; his speech somewhat indistinct. His gestures are slow; the unhealthy pallor of his complexion indicates a man whose constitution is not robust. He dresses in white, gray, and black. A long muslin scarf that's wrapped in folds about his huge spheroid turban and fully covering him down to his belt gives him the look of a marabout. He speaks little, asking questions in a low voice. He doesn't look straight at those brought before the court unless the question really merits his attention, listening most of the time somewhat distractedly, his elbow resting on the cushions, half meditating, half dreaming. He offers the appearance of a man you might share small confidences with.

Four or five scribes, a process server armed with a stick, and a handsome, mild-looking judge, representing in his person the court and authority, jurisprudence, and the law: that sums up the magistrature. No barristers or lawyers, no public prosecutor; no postponements, no procedures to follow, no complications, no dilatoriness. You go in with your opponent and sit down on the floor next to him. Each in turn tells his story and the contradictory presentations make up both the arguments and the investigation. Nothing could be more summary. It's more or less what a justice of the peace does, in other words, the most logical, humane, most accurate laying down of the law. If it's true that the first goal of justice should be to conciliate, he really merits our appellation "justice of the peace." When agreement is impossible the cadi like Solomon pronounces judgment derived from his own wisdom and conscience.

Women don't enter the courtroom proper for leading to the hearing room are two open galleries reserved for them. They communicate with the tribunal through a window with grillwork at the height of your elbow. A woman (who remains veiled) can at most insert her fingers through the grillwork of bars and help her case along with a brief pantomime.

The day I became acquainted with the judicial system that I've been describing to you, there was appropriately a case pending between a woman and her husband. It concerned a request for divorce. Behind the grilled opening and completely invisible underneath her veils, the aggrieved party set out nevertheless with great readiness her scarcely mentionable grievances and told without batting an eye the history of her married life, which would be impossible to render here. The husband, whom the cadi had just interrogated, looked ingenuous as he listened to what she said about him. The cadi, however, did not judge the marriage to be as desperate as the impatient wife made out. On the contrary, he advised them to try to get along better than in the past, putting the case off until the following year.

Above this first level of jurisdiction is the mufti, who as a last resort can pass judgment. He's a very old man whom I run into as he strolls about the bazaar wearing a reddish caftan, a green coat, and yellow babouches, head wrapped in a veil of purple-colored silk. The small lodge that he occupies next to the cadi is a sort of tomblike structure that's quite small, very quiet, and dimly lit. To me the most religious respect surrounded this sanctuary of high justice. Within it well toward the rear under the cupola the old man dozed as if he were a magus; his age and the high seriousness of the spot gave him a quite august look. When a plaintiff has lost his case he only has to cross the courtyard to go from court of first instance to appeals court. All is not over with when he's made use of both these jurisdictions. For those whom the law of men has displeased a final recourse remains: that's to call upon heavenly justice and so go to the mosque to make an appeal before God.

January 12

THE RAIN has come. Around three in the afternoon it began with a few scattered large drops. I was ending my walk just as this hopeful sign the whole countryside had been begging for manifested itself, not without effort, out of a stormy yet obstinately arid sky. I wasn't surprised for I'd gone out to wait for it. For eight days the weather had been getting ready for the change. The air was too restless to remain still for long and the sky was of a peculiar blue that prevented you from believing the fine days could continue. These are subtleties that with a little practice you recognize. Deep inside as well I felt the rain coming, a premonition that was far from being illusory.

I was getting to a field that an Arab farmer in a short tunic was planting in barley; he was finishing covering over the last rows, pushing along a small primitive plow hitched to two thin cows. Seeing that the weather was just right for planting, he was exhorting his animals, hurrying so that he might finish off before nightfall, without a doubt figuring that the next day would be too late. At the end of the already plowed field, two children, also Arabs, were setting fire to large mountains of weeds that sent up billows of acrid-smelling smoke. I recognized right there with some surprise the common smell of burned-over fields in France, this being the first slight tangible indication of autumn.

I sat down and looked at this field crisscrossed with brown furrows where I observed two things rather rare in this carefree country: an Arab plow in use and local children sharing with their father the tasks involved in farming. The small cows were not yoked together but harnessed under and around their forequarters, pulling with their shoulders like horses, breathing as if exhausted even though the task was not difficult, the mere breaking of the ground's surface.

Just at that moment I noticed the smoke, which up till then had lain heavy on the air, turn about. A slight breeze, but cool, came out of the west; it followed where the vineyards begin, and as it progressed gave out the sound of the wings of a very large bird. It was as if the countryside was surprised for one after the other in a sudden movement all the trees in the plain were trembling on account of it. That lasted just an instant. The gust over, all was unrelieved calm once more. That's when the first drops of rain fell.

Nothing was recognizable anymore—not Algiers, which appeared as a colorless amphitheater, nor the Turkish houses as white as sheets—they lost their shape by not possessing any shadows—or the sea that was now livid, or the trees in the Sahel that were now a faded green. Even though the air was still tepid you could feel a rush of damp cool. All at the same time, in the villages and on the farms, the chimneys started smoking as everyone reacted to the same news, making ready right off for winter. Pigeons scattered about the countryside returned two by two to their lofts as hens, much upset, did to their coops. On the other hand, groups of geese hurried out into the farmyards and domesticated ducks flapped their wings joyously as they caught the rain, letting out quacks of dismay at the edge of the dried-out reservoirs. Blackbirds flew from tree to tree calling to each other with their twilight song. Even though the sun was above the horizon they were already bedding down, providentially, deep within the hedges. I heard the thrushes singing, being the first ones perhaps that winter had entrusted with its message; flocks of starlings from out of the prairies arrived in closed-in legions to secure for themselves shelter close to the hills.

Summer was indeed winding down. It was ending without violence, under a soft, drab sky, without storms and with only beneficial downpours. Was it the last good-bye of the season that was now past? Was it the first present of a winter that wanted to have its arrival feted, thus heralding it with blessings?

IT'S COMING straight down. The wind is weak but comes right out of the west, which is a bad sign at this time of year. The sea is roiling. I hear the roar of the open sea on a moonless night without stars, weighed down with clouds and made denser yet by the sheets of rain. Rather than the sole tossing of the waves, there's also a kind of interior groan. You'd think that the depths were being set in motion by a storm climbing to the surface from the very bottom. There isn't the slightest noise throughout the countryside, which seems dead or in deepest sleep. For a long time now the fires have been out everywhere, even in that part of the city's outskirts that I can see from my window. Good-bye blue sky, good-bye sun, good-bye everything that seemed inalterable.

January 13

THE RAIN continues. Hour by hour the wind only gets stronger, steady now from its winter quarter; it begins to churn up the water in the bay. The coast has disappeared within the movement of the sea, marked only by rapid whitish jets of spray. The squall is magnified with each passing minute, shrinking the horizon as it shuts it out with an almost impenetrable layer that hangs vertically like a curtain. The countryside is as empty as the sea; it's inundated, for the earth, which has been taken by surprise by this sudden watering, hasn't been able to absorb it quickly enough. Water runs down roads turned into streams and lingers on the surface of the prairies; the Hamma is one long swamp. You can see terrified birds crossing the mud-colored sky like shadows. Unable to master the wind or keep flying for any length of time, they plunge as if dead into the first shrub that comes along. The olive trees now are really sorrowful in that rain; in the wind that shreds their scant leafage, beating at them as if with a lash, they've come to look like trees up north. All traffic, apparently, is suspended; no one has yet to appear on the roads hereabout. Before resuming his activities everyone waits for the squall to subside or for the winter season to make itself recognizable through steadier attributes.

I visited my garden—it's a small pond—then the farm where the dog is asleep in his kennel. The horses in their stalls are sleeping too, and the pigeons gently coo in the farthest corners of the open-ended dovecote.

I saw my neighbor Monsieur Adam standing by the entrance to his house that's now in ruins. His flock of chickens take comfort as they can by pecking grain they've missed on the worn windowsills. Monsieur Adam was smoking his German pipe, waiting in sadness for the end of the rain as well as that of his exile. I blocked the tiniest apertures in my dwelling. To inaugurate the season that was beginning I lit a big fire of fragrant logs. Here I am, just as in France, my feet toward the fire, quite amazed at the change that's occurred about me in the past twenty-four hours. I'm well aware that I'll be paying with a few annoyances for pleasures that were intense. Furthermore, my imprisonment—and that's what it is—will last only as long as I want it to. All depends on the burden of solitude.

January 18

FOR FIVE days now I've witnessed something less formidable yet just as desperate as a flood. The sky is dark, as is the sea; there's almost no daylight and there's a roar as monotonous, yet as relaxing, as silence, then rain and more rain coming down on a marshland and enormous cataracts heading down to the sea. The shutters, not made for such an assault, threatened to burst open at each renewed effort of the wind. The windows gave, almost about to break, and my house shook like an uprooted tree. The really terrifying thing to hear and see, when you're able, is the sea.

end of January

THE SUN has yet to come back out and the sky is dull. Sorrowful colors disfigure this beautiful land, freshly in leaf in spite of winter —happy land whose sole expression normally is a smile. The wind continues to blow. The sea heaves sighs of vexation as the forlorn waters churn.

Do you know the hardest thing to accept in this dark picture? Its composition is a confusion of falling rain, tumbling waves, shooting spray and traveling clouds that nowhere reveals any equilibrium. You continue to watch ill-defined things coming and going; they come into balance only to be upset in the perpetual rolling that appears unable ever to quiet down. There's nothing to catch the eye's attention, to give it a rest, or to satisfy it by fixing it on points of reference. You see a floating surface and an undecided perspective of unmanageable forms. Everything is moving and there's not one feature that doesn't vanish as soon as it materializes. For me a minor kind of agony and something I was ignorant of.

If this were to continue, I'd leave Mustapha for the sea is unbearable when no longer calm. I don't look at it anymore as I wait, trying not to hear it and doing what I can to forget about it. I'm working and console myself with clear colors, rigid forms, and well-defined lines. Gaiety isn't what pleases me in light. What delights me is the precision it lends to contours. Of all the attributes that go with grandeur the most beautiful as far as I'm concerned is immobility. To put it another way, I have a genuine fondness for things that last; I can only consider with some passion things that are stationary.

Mustapha d'Alger

I DON'T KNOW whether winter is over, but the weather is very beautiful.

The landscape is transfigured and the entire countryside is green again. While I maligned winter, today it gives witness to its charity. Thanks to the prodigious quantity of rain that's fallen, we now have replenished springs, fields brought back to life, trees swelling with sap, the earth's tiniest veins supplied with water for a year. There's no plot of ground that's so depleted that it's not recovered a bountiful prairie-like fertility and no abandoned fields that haven't shot up with abundant good grass for grazing. An immense stretch that's the color of hope continues on beyond the villages, the farms, and the main roads from the wall around Algiers all the way to the mountains of Kabylia. There massive reserves of snow are stocked for the first days of great heat. Crops vanish in the middle of that unchanging steppe—sheaths of wheat will be noticeable only as they yellow. Sheep have been put out to graze in the hippodrome where the cavalry no longer practices. The almond trees are in bloom and along the damp ditches where they have been herded the camels devour the young shoots of the ash trees.

The land was already springlike, waiting only for such a day to find itself in complete harmony with the weather; and here the spring is never that far away. The season can change with the wind. When it turns to the north, it's winter, which only has the sea to cross. Once the new season decides to come it's here in just a few minutes along with the heat the Sahara exhales. The wind is so weak today that the thinnest plumes of smoke bend hardly at all; but from that first breath you inhale you guess both at where it's coming from and what it promises. It brings the first news of spring; I can attest that there's not a blade of grass in this land that hadn't been apprised of this since daybreak.

As if a recuperating patient, I took advantage of this brief and perhaps short-lived moment of compassion to take a walk. No destination in mind, I let chance decide, taking the first road to come along. I went along slowly and easily, modeling myself on the sick man whose return to good health is first signaled by his surprise at everything he sees, his silent joy in being alive. Some very simple things I saw delighted me, but the major event that day was the weather. Are you aware, my friend, of the incalculable effects that result when the barometer goes up or down? Have you ever noticed to what extent this little instrument rules us?

Perhaps all of us while alive live dependent on certain occult forces whose actions we are subjected to without our either acknowledging them or being able to pin them down. Perhaps buried in the destiny of us all are miserable little secrets that we don't talk about out of fear of confessing our enslavement, thereby humiliating in the presence of mere matter a human soul pretending to be free. As far as I'm concerned, after this long imprisonment, after a month of chatting face-to-face with my shadow, the slightest stirring in my brain becomes an adventure; a sensation getting through from the outside is as good as an anecdote. And don't be surprised if I end up considering it an uncommon pleasure to be moved by something!

I followed the coastal road, which farther on becomes a main artery for commerce since it takes you on into Kabylia. Right now it's quite deserted. You'll only encounter the rare Arab on foot coming back from the market with a meager convoy of beasts, some empty *tellis* (duffel bags), pack saddles, and bunches of rope hanging loosely around shabby harnesses, or instead—and rarer yet— Maltese on the prowl, who are half peasants and half sea hands. After every storm they prey upon the coast, grabbing what they can from the wreckage. No one was in the fields. The farms have nothing to do once they've been sown: first the rain and then the sun take care of the rest. The sky was gray, very calm to the farthest horizons just what the weather-beaten people in my part of the country and yours call "young lady weather."

Halfway to Maison Carrée, I sat down on a promontory off to

one side. If there hadn't been lots of aloes and cactus, I could have believed I was four hundred leagues from Africa, on a shore that stands as high and empty as this one and where you look out at a sea that's not this one. The impression was the same, the grandeur equivalent. That day the Mediterranean resembled the Atlantic Ocean. It was light in color and at long intervals propelled groups of large, sad waves with little strength; reacting to the calm air, they slackened hour by hour. Off toward Matiflou you now could hardly hear the still perceivable rumble of a storm kept out to sea by a contrary wind. At my feet, and so close to the waves that you'd have thought they were going to engulf them, some seabirds hopped about, just like those we have in France, with gray plumage and pointed wings. Like all the inhabitants of sandy stretches, they get about on stilts; their beaks, which are as sharp as pikes, are incessantly pecking the spongy soil along the beach. Their cry, made up of a small sigh as negligible as a noise can be, seems to have been given them as a gauge to measure by its weakness the huge noise of the sea. Nothing is more melancholy yet more arresting than this little bird who lives, runs, and sings two inches from the sea, never leaving it, either to live on land or venture on long journeys. At most and only when chased away, he'll cross the narrow bays, never distancing himself from that thin strip of moist sand where his life is passed. When a wave comes in, he opens his wings to avoid it. Where does he hide when it storms? He's no longer there but is a witness. He lets the big commotion calm down, and as soon as the coast become habitable again he flirts with the sea once more.

I headed home toward nightfall over darkened roads shrouded in the abundant moisture that was descending. I couldn't make out the sea any longer—I heard it. Algiers was starry with lights. Everywhere a dwelling was hid the countryside was marked by a red light. As I got to the cavalry training grounds, I was vaguely aware of the outline of my house and I saw my lighted lantern that shone through the open window.

Between Sea and Sahara I

JUST TODAY I've received the following letter:

"They've told me that you're back. I've been at Blidah for three days and expect to stay here a week or two to rest up my old horse who's quite done in. If nothing's detaining you there, I'll expect you. This very morning I saw a small house near the orange groves that would be to my taste as well as yours.

"In remembrance of the past that made us fellow travelers, and anticipating the future, I send you fond best wishes.

"BOU-DJABA

"My address: rue des Koulouglis, c/o Bou-Dhiaf."

I'll remind you once more in case you've forgotten that this is a friend of mine (in French, Louis Vandell). Right now I'm readying my baggage looking toward being away for an indefinite period. I hereby end my journal from Mustapha, a little embarrassed that it's so empty. Good night. I'm leaving tomorrow morning with the seven o'clock stagecoach.

2

Blidah

I'M WRITING YOU from here in Blidah, where I've found quarters and set myself up. It was a speedy trip in a stagecoach in which everyone except me spoke Provençal, so that I didn't have to say a single word during the five hours it took. The option of keeping quiet is the first freedom that I insist upon when traveling, and I wish it were written down in a special article of human rights that everyone is required to respect.

I hardly had time to glimpse Bir-Mandréis as the team galloped across the hills slashed by ravines. The horses, however, are always exhausted after a climb followed by the corkscrew descent from the Sahel and usually catch their breath for three minutes by the pretty Arab fountain at Bir-Kradem. It's been pointed and restored without altering its style. Examining that elegant marble facade gilded by the sun, I thought of it as an old friend bringing back old memories of Africa dating from our first trip.

The morning was cool, the air brisk, and the sky of an admirably clear, unchanging blueness. I was able to take in and in a flash assess the size of the magnificent plain that along with Sicily was the granary of the Romans and will be ours when it has its own legions of farmhands. I'm fond of the plains—this one is the most impressive if not one of the most vast that I've ever seen. Even if you can cross it, as in France, over a long paved road bearing the marks of civilization in its ruts and along which you encounter relay posts and villages and from time to time farms with people, it is all the same a vast solitary stretch where man's handiwork is imperceptible, the tallest trees sinking below the different levels of the horizon. It's mysterious like all horizons; you can only make out distinctly the farthest reaches. To the right is the low horizontal of the Sahel, to the rear the mountains of Milianah lost in pale blues, and to the left the lofty escarpment of the Atlas range hung in somber green, snow on all the peaks. There wasn't a cloud about that sparkling ridge; you could just make out halfway up the side some leftover mists, caused by evaporation in the ravines, that rolled up in white puffs like smoke out of a cannon. The low part of the plain is hidden under water, the marsh of Oued-el-Laleg, which is hardly damp in summertime, having inundated the countryside for two leagues around.

Returning to Bouffarick, I found it booming. Gone the sick and the feverish. These days, Europeans are healthier there than elsewhere and those who have come down with the fever even prefer to go there to convalesce. While so many men were dying there, having been poisoned from breathing the vapors from both the stagnant water and the turned-over soil, the trees, which live on what kills us, went on growing exuberantly as if in manure. Just imagine now a Norman orchard planted to poplars, aspens, willows, well-cared-for, fertile and with lots of fruit, filled with the odor of stables, filled with country activity—real country and real country folk. We no longer think about the past of this little place whose richness is now being developed so systematically. We forget that to make it ours ten years of warfare against the Arabs and twenty years of struggle with the climate—much more of a killer than the fighting—were necessary. A traveler remembers these things only when he passes near the cemeteries or when he stops in Beni-Mered by the column erected to honor Sergeant Blandan.[13] The real history of the colony is, here as everywhere, entrusted to tombs. Such heroism, my friend, on the part of the known and unknown, almost all of whom are already forgotten yet not one of whom lived in vain.

By eleven I was in Blidah. There I found Vandell, who after sending me his letter had been expecting my arrival with each succeeding coach. I recognized from a distance his yellowish cap, the same one he was wearing four years ago. He was smoking his small pipe, whose cherry wood stem is without a mouthpiece. His whole person had kept that same slightly bizarre air that is as hard to forget as it is to define.

I rented the house that Vandell proposed, and it was agreed that together we would camp there. The house is situated at the very end of the town in a deserted spot planted with orange trees; the ramparts' fortified walls are all that separate it from the plantations of orange trees. On one side we have the view of the plain and on the other the mountain, which is so close, dominating from on high the city that lies at its feet. We feel we could touch it with our hands. Even though the terrace, which is in need of repair, lets the rain in, our lodgings appear quite habitable. A stream surfaces near the door, and you can hear a slight rustling noise over gravel from the running water. Six feet from there a large cypress tree is growing: just a trunk and some leaves at the top coming to a point. All day long, top to bottom, it gets the sun, which goes full circle around the tree whose shadow outlines on the flatness of the ground a perfectly regular sundial. If I gave it a face with some pebbles, I'd have my own clock.

Blidah, February

VANDELL hasn't changed his habits any more than he has his physiognomy or dress. He resembles no one and yet resembles, and always will, himself: he's a singular person who doesn't change. There is, however, some gray in his hair, which he keeps very short, and in his beard, which on the contrary, he lets grow as it will; but those changes are almost invisible. His face is now of the sort that has nothing left to lose either in rosiness or plumpness. As brown as a white man can be and as thin as is possible for a man in good health, this traveler is hard-pressed by fatigue, the effects of the burning sun as well as the years, but being in good shape can daunt the latter with certainty. He no longer looks to have ever been young. You can never figure in what way he grows older; from now on I'd defy anyone to affix an age to him. Always healthy, so much more so since he's thin, alert, and has excellent legs like the walker he is, he has out of necessity also become a so-so horseman. Vandell takes no particular care of what he calls his "envelope" except whatever is of use to it for the services he expects of it, which as you might imagine, are excessive. His main concern is to diminish the "inside" and develop the "outside"; in other words, to shrink his muscles and thicken his skin. He has on this subject a practical philosophy that's his very own. "Isn't it pitiable," he told me one day, "that cheap cloth such as I'm wearing is tougher than a man's skin, which was made by a healthy human couple? But don't worry, I'll find out how to resist the elements, becoming no longer sensitive to pain, long-wearing and resilient like cow hide." Judging by his face and his hands, he has already succeeded. Today I told him, "I think, my friend, that you're the one who will wear out time. Life may bite you, yet it's like a serpent that bites a metal file."

"That doesn't alter the fact," he replied uneasily, "that the works are weary." By "the works" Vandell means his brain and the levers of his intellectual processes. This is his way of playing with words out of whatever kind of bashful respect for ideas. Deep down he's very intelligent as solitary people can be.

Did I ever tell you how I knew Vandell? It was during my second voyage here, during a trip I was taking to the southern parts. We were crossing a mountainous and wooded stretch in a caravan; the convoy was made up of mules rather than camels. All the long springtime day that cavalcade of hard hooves had been tramping the narrow stony paths of the mountain; it must have been five o'clock and we were nearing our bivouac. The caravan in its entirety was coming out onto a plateau covered by low copse and shrubs that was devoid of roads but crisscrossed by narrow clearings. We went out on to it one by one, each one counting on his mount to follow instinctively by smelling the tracks of the riders in the lead. I was walking in the rear guard, and in any case, my horse was one of those who in such a situation have no need to be led. He started neighing and became nervous. Beyond the thickets I could see a rider coming into view whom I did not recognize as one of our own. The newcomer was a tall young man dressed for travel and mounted on an extremely thin beast of a dirty white with an inferior harness in the Arab style. The rider too was thin—scrawny and as sunburned as a Saharan. The sole detail of note that redeemed the penury manifest in his accoutrements and that called up someone more or less civilized was that instead of a weapon slung across his shoulder he carried something like a long barometer inside a leather sheath plus a voluminous tin cylinder.

"Excuse me, sir," he said, keeping his distance, "Does your horse excite easily in the presence of a mare?"

"Very easily, sir, as a rule," was my reply.

"In that case, I'll go on ahead of you."

Without waiting further he gave his mount a tap with his crop and set her trotting. He rode English style, not moving in the saddle, just applying pressure on the broad Arab stirrups with a slight movement of the knees. I saw him disappear, encased to just above the waist by the deep backrest of the saddle, and afterward heard for two or three minutes the regular noise of the barometer knocking against his specimen case.

When we got to the bivouac I met up with this individual again; he was smoking his pipe and chatting. We were introduced to each other; his name was Monsieur Louis Vandell. I'd heard a lot about him. He was mentioned everywhere for his travel adventures and the singular way he lived. I was able to tell him quite sincerely how much I valued the chance to meet him. That very evening at the bivouac we got to know each other. I put him up since I had the least amount of baggage and my tent therefore the most room. In the tent he put his greatcoat, or rather his black burnoose in which he rolled up and lashed with straps his Arab saddle and his instruments. This was his bed, covering, and pillow. It was a magnificent night spent almost entirely listening to him.

"You see," he said, "this land is mine: it has adopted me and to it I owe unique freedom and an unparalleled life. I'll pay back this bounty, if I can, with a modest piece of work composed during my leisure time. Most people think that I'm a just a wanderer but perhaps I'll prove one day that I haven't completely wasted my time. This barometer, which earned me the Arab name Bou-Djaba (the gun barrel man), seems more valuable in my hands than a real rifle."

He was up at dawn and called his mare that he had quite simply turned loose in the encampment. He saddled and harnessed her himself having first given her a bit of barley left in one of the pockets of his *djebira* (saddle bag), the others being full of rock samples. We broke camp, Vandell accompanying us until we stopped for our main break. From time to time he would get down whenever he found a vertical support that suited him: he'd hang his barometer from it, jotting down the reading in an old much-worn notebook. Then he would quicken the pace of his mount (that never went very fast) and catch up with the end of the convoy.

"Here I'll leave you," he said when we remounted for the afternoon stage. "I intend to pass the night over there where you see that mountain shaped like an eagle's beak."

Then he stretched out his hand, saying, "I'd like to give you something from me as a keepsake."

He pulled out of his pocket and gave me a black licorice stick that he broke in two and half a length of rope.

"These are to quench your thirst when you're feeling really thirsty and to mend your harness if the heat causes any of your straps to break. They may be a help to you in a jam. Good-bye for

Blidah

77

now, for unless you're planning to leave the country soon, we'll probably see each other again."

"Good-bye!" I said, and cordially shook his hand. Our horses, which during that time had been getting to know each other, took heed from our spurs, and we went our ways. We were in the plain; for a good hour I could see the white haunches of his horse and his specimen case shining in the sun like a mirror.

Just as he predicted, I've seen him twice since then on this trip. The first was at the edge of a spring; he was all alone taking the midday break. The second was in a *douar* where we were encamped; he himself came along near midnight. The dogs were making a great racket, out of which I heard hooves of a horse that then stopped. Two minutes later someone lifted the flap of my tent and I saw Vandell appear. He was straightening out a little-known point of history concerning the third Roman legion's stay in the province; he'd been prowling thereabouts for a month.

Today as then he's still knocking about the country far away as always from the towns and off well-traveled roads, always alone, and coming into a *douar* only to sleep. To begin with, as I've told you, he's indifferent to the time of year for he's as little bothered by extreme cold as by extreme heat. He's also so organized his work to be able to use spring and fall for long expeditions and summer for brief trips encompassing one area. Winter is reserved for what he calls his desk work, meaning that during the big rains he holes up in the first *douar* he comes to. He'll stay their a week or two, if necessary, wrapped up in his burnoose, writing. From time to time he gathers together the materials he's collected, rather complicated and diverse and sometimes quite abundant, and deposits them at the nearest outpost with a trusted friend. In keeping with this practice he's scattered his treasures in the four corners of Algeria and when the day comes that he makes up his mind to assemble them he will have to undertake a final voyage that won't be the shortest he's made.

Vandell has gone everywhere where an intrepid and innocuous

traveler can go. He's seen everything that's worth seeing; he knows everything about the three provinces that an encyclopedic memory is capable of retaining. Thanks to the range of what he knows, the variety of services that he can dispense, but above all thanks to the quirkiness of his ways and the strangeness of his life, he's as well received by the Arabs as a dervish combined with a *theb* (medical doctor) can be. He also shows up without risking any harm in places a battalion would never go, fearing nothing day or night save the inconvenience of a pickpocket. Even there, his penury is his protection.

In fact, he told me on that subject, "The surest thing is to offer a temptation to no one: 'A thousand knights aren't capable of stripping a naked man.'"

He had been camping only a few leagues from Taguin when the Duke of Aumale's[14] column surprised the *smala*. He thus was present at the siege of Zaatcha, taking part only as a spectator. Since then, in fact just recently, as he was making his way one day toward the territory of the Ouled-Nayl between Djelfa and Chareff, an army was assembling before El-Aghouat. Straightaway, fearing he might be too late, he doubled his pace to reach the top of the range of hills just as the first cannon shots of the siege were fired. At that point, and he's the one who told me this, he dismounted and from up in his observatory viewed the battle as comfortably as one might wish. I saw sketches from his folder he'd done that day. He began by putting down the plan of the city and the panorama of the site of the action; then, keeping up with the maneuvers which he could make out very well, he indicated, using unbroken and dotted lines with a pencil, the movements of the attacking elements and the positions of the battalions from moment to moment. Right as a cannon was fired, from either the town or the French batteries, leaving a large distinct cloud of smoke, the sketcher depicted the rapid explosion and its exact shape by gently rubbing with a white drawing pencil. He decamped once the town had been taken. He went down into it as soon as it was possible;

Blidah

this time he was armed with a rifle someone lent him. When he had seen what he wanted and taken note of what seemed useful he left, setting off once more toward the north, boldly heading straight across the territory of the Ouled-Nayl to Bouçada.

"By the way," I asked him today, "how do you happen to be in Blidah?"

"Just chance, my dear friend. When I was ten leagues from here up in the mountains and while I was apparently dozing, my mare smelled a stable a distance away and turned to the left instead of to the right, taking me up to the entrance of the ravine." He added cheerfully that he really didn't mind after all, and the poor beast didn't either.

Blidah, February

"While strangers call you a small city (Blidah),
I'm from there, I call you a small rose (ourida)."

A DISTICH like a love song is all that's left of Blidah: a charming name that rhymes with "rose." The city no longer exists. From the lips of Arabs the name still sounds like a tender, much-missed memory of delights from days gone by.

Blidah actually was the city par excellence of roses, jasmine, and women. From the plain's edge where you could make out its towers and white houses half-hidden in a forest of trees with golden fruit, just across from "Koleah the Holy," it looked like the foretold picture of the allowable, promised joys of paradise. Within it were evergreen gardens, tree-lined streets shadier than woods, imposing cafés filled with music, small houses sheltering refined pleasures, and everywhere water—delightful water. Finally, to envelop the total well-being of this sensual people, there was the continual breath of the orange trees in bloom making the atmosphere seem like perfume. They made fragrant essences there and sold jewelry. Warriors came to take their ease and the young to learn of vice. Marabouts, who would have been out of place, lived off in the mountains. In this place mosques stood as reminders, like beads in the hands of a debauched man.

Today Blidah resembles in every way a Moorish woman, such as you see about the city, who once was beautiful and no longer is. She dresses in the European style with a hat in the worst taste, a dress that's badly made, and gloves that have seen better days: no more shaded streets, no more cafés, three-quarters of the houses destroyed and replaced by European structures. There are immense barracks, colonial streets, and instead of Arab life, there's camp life, the least mysterious of any, most specially in the pursuit of pleasure. What the war began, peace ended. The day when Blidah no longer has anything that's Arab it will become once again a very lovely city. Perhaps the new Blidah will dispel the memory of the old one when those that miss her will themselves have gone on.

Moreover, there will be so many things remaining to make it beautiful and prosperous. Above all, its location is such that even if an earthquake were to demolish the present city it would be rebuilt. Then there's fertile soil and clear water now distributed better than ever and which French industry makes use of—where the Arabs saw only an attraction we find a moneymaker. Right at the gates of the city there's the splendid plain and the mountain looking down. The climate is very mild with just enough winter to help with European crops and a summer that is adapted to tropical ones. The air is healthy, winds off the desert are rare. Those that come off the sea are unimpeded from either the east or west passing straight from full north. On the horizon are three hundred thousand hectares of land awaiting the plow; and finally, something of a luxury, orange groves. It's said they are much diminished but they still account for that garden of the Hesperides being the main source of oranges. Although what was delightful in this pleasure spot has vanished, we must comfort ourselves with the spectacle of what is of use. I reiterate that the future will wipe out the past. Most of all it will excuse the present, which, it should be stated without being unjust, is in need of being excused.

In the meantime, I wander about the center of this ungainly city, not yet able to visualize what it will be and seeking what it has stopped being, imagining both with difficulty. I spend time at the barber's; I chat with the sellers of fodder and visit the French market to see the first flowers. I also go to the Arab market to observe the black women, tribal folk, and mountain people who come down every morning, driving before them herds of donkeys burdened with firewood and charcoal. There are still cafés, modern ones—and what cafés! The members of the indigenous police force are about the only thing out of the ordinary there. They're nicely gotten up, dressed Turkish style. As elsewhere in the world they carry two insignias of the law's repressive force, a stick and a dagger, the latter in lieu of a sword.

Sometimes a magistrate, a cadi or some such, wearing a long coat will be sitting quite relaxed drinking his coffee. Three things are his constant companions never leaving his hands: his jasmine-scented water pipe, his beads, and his Tunisian handkerchief. People passing present their respects and the *kaouadgi* (waiter) kisses him on the shoulder. if by chance the clientele is particularly numerous or select, the *kaouadgi* will appear with rose, jasmine, or benzoin water in a flacon whose stopper has holes like that of a pepper shaker. He makes the rounds of those seated and with great dignity as if he were conducting a ceremony sprinkles the faces and clothes with a fine spray of scent. That gallant offering usually costs some small change offered as a tip. From time to time I treat myself and leave town by the Bab-el-Sebt where I can all of a sudden behold the plain as if it were my first time seeing it. The view of the horizon is noteworthy for its breadth, grandeur, and nobility. A traveler remains steadfastly attached to it even after having seen that rarest of pictures, the "Tomb of the Christian Woman" (Kouber-er-Roumia)[15] facing Blidah. It's situated between Lake Haloûla and the stubby mass of Chenoûa mountain. It takes in the Masafran, the "stream with golden water," that crossing the Sahel makes its exit through a narrow gap where the sea can be glimpsed; Koleah, which is all white, creating an odd kind of sparkle on the brown slopes; and to the left in a broad row the mountains of Milianah with their three tiers enclosing the enormous plain with a somber azure curtain shot with silver. It's all most beautifully composed as well as being blessed with entrancing names. This is the spot, my friend, where in the joy of coming here for the first time and finally seeing the real land of the Arabs, having imagined it for so long, together we exclaimed, "Oh, Palestine!"

There's one time of day in this city in ruins that I prefer to the hours of great luminousness—it even resigns me to its present state —and that's the evening as night falls, that brief moment of uncertainty following right after day, preceding darkness. Shadows descend and are accompanied at this time of year by a thick fog half wiping out, dabbing with blue the end of even the shortest streets. The pavement is wet, your feet slipping about some among the half shadows in those parts of the city which are badly lit. The side of city toward the setting sun is awash in violet flashes of light. The buildings have something odd in their look, and as the sky loses its coloring it seems to make them evaporate one by one. You're only vaguely aware of all those strange people coming home, blocking—shrinking—the streets where they live. You hear around you people talking in a guttural language that's a little bizarre; you can make out the voices of the women, which are softer and those of the children, which are shriller. Young girls go by bearing wooden trays of bread; they call out *"Balek!"*—as they duck among the crowd. Not being able to distinguish any special features, you brush up against veiled women, who become recognizable by the whiteness of their dress; they seem to slip away. If you at all have a taste for wondering and dreaming, it's possible to recreate a society that's long gone. You're allowed to suppose many things that no longer exist in the realm of both art and gallantry.

I HADN'T been expecting at all what happened to me. I ran into that unknown Moorish woman from the crossroads of Sid-Mohammed-el-Schériff. She lives in Blidah, and to put things like a true Frenchman, I have permission to appear tomorrow at noon where she lives.

Yesterday around two there was drum playing in a small street in the neighborhood. In addition to the noise of sticks of wood striking tender hides, the jangling of iron crotals and singers' voices reached us from off the terraces.

Vandell asked, "Do you want to hear a little music?"

I replied, "By all means, and as this performance by a group of blacks is all we're going to get, let's go!"

I must note here that Vandell, who was very indulgent as far as Arabs were concerned, has a hard time excusing them for not being musically inclined.

"Here's what they claim to believe," he commented to me while on our way. They are so filled with themselves that they think that the blooms of certain flowers, in particular those of mullein and artemisia, fall from their stems when they play their *mizmounes*. It's an old Latin conceit that was somehow passed down to them:

> "Ilicibus glandes, cantataque vitibus uva
> Decidit . . ."[16]

A section of the wall on the street side of the house the sounds were coming from was missing. We could see through a big gap at about the height of a windowsill what was going on almost as well as if we had gone inside. It was a small family party with every-body joining in. They formed a circle around the entrance to a low-ceilinged room. A pretty young black woman was presiding over the gathering, which no doubt was being held in her honor. Her breasts were uncovered as she nursed her naked baby. Two Moorish women squatting on rugs each held big iron crotals, which were much too big for their small hands. Two blacks were singing and beating on drums. A third one stood a few feet away from the nursing mother; half-clothed, no hat, belt flying, he performed frenzied dances in honor of the newborn. The courtyard was small, almost entirely covered over by a huge leafless fig tree. Its branches were thick and knotted, thus able by their multiplicity to shade the pavement. The tree's trunk rose out of a big puddle of stagnant water in which ducks paddled. There were also chickens tied in twos with a piece of string around a leg. Like prisoners who weren't felt to be trustworthy, they circled around a manure heap, very put out by their fetters. Unable to agree, each one pulled the string in the direction it wanted. As you can see, it was a kind of Flemish scene as homey as it could be. I wouldn't have composed the picture like that—I recount exactly what I saw.

A small child, who wasn't taking part in the occasion, saw us and came to open the door. There were brief greetings in the form of hand waving so as not to interrupt the festivities one minute. The dancer energized his dance, stepping up the tempo and beating on his gong with even greater vigor and gusto, having as he now did two foreigners watching. He was beside himself, bathed in sweat, looking just like bronze that's been sprinkled with water.

The Moorish women, who were unveiled, were pretty and well-dressed in winter clothes with a long-sleeved caftan over the bodice. The design of the silk had a profusion of flowers and gold. Their whole person was so imbibed with scent, they gave off an intolerable odor of amber. For a whole hour none of us said a word. The newborn, who whimpered as he worried the nursing mother's splendid breasts, was the only voice to be heard. Finally, as was only natural, the man was first to be tired. The music then halted and the festivities ended as festivities of that sort do since, unbelievably, fatigue always precedes boredom. We took our leave of the family of the house, and the Moorish women, who were also only guests like us, made ready to go. When they had covered themselves with their *haiks* and adjusted their white cotton veils, and as they passed in front of us as regally veiled as on the street, Vandell greeted them in Arabic and I imitated him. The smaller and slimmer of the two women said, "Good-bye, sir," in French to me. I recognized that "Good-bye, sir" from the crossroads in Algiers. This time old Abdallah wasn't there, and without waiting to think things over, I followed them.

"Do you know who you're dealing with?" asked Vandell.

"I can guess," was my answer, "but I have my reasons, which I'll tell you later, for being interested in the one who said 'Good-bye.'"

The two women parted at the end of the street. I let her friend go on a bit and then followed the other one. She never turned her head, at least as far as I could tell. After a few turns she arrived at her house. The neighborhood was deserted—an Arab street, an Arab house. She pushed the heavy door, leaning on it with her whole body, and disappeared. I was following in her footsteps and saw the door close by its own weight, vibrating on its hinges. Since they hadn't put back the crosspiece, there was still something of a draft, which at intervals would make the door open just a crack. I waited a couple of seconds, uncertain as to what I would do when it swung again. The woman was before me. Through where her veil dipped she was gazing at me, but of her eyes I could only see two luminous, motionless diamond-like dots.

"Don't come in," she told me in *sabir*, that is, in a barbaric version of Italian. "Come instead tomorrow at noon."

I must admit, my friend, that I was taken aback by this ready cordiality. I repeated, "Tomorrow at noon."

Vandell was my lookout at the end of street.

"So?" he said.

"So, I'm coming back tomorrow!'"

I quickly filled him in about our first encounter. He knows Sid-Abdallah—who doesn't know him! That merchant is an upright person whose loyalty you can count on. His remark to "watch out" was meant as a piece of advice.

"As for the woman," Vandell added, "if you want to find out about her, let's seek out Hassan the barber. We'll get him to talk, that is, if he's feeling like being indiscreet."

Does an inquiry have much point in a matter of such middling interest?

YESTERDAY afternoon Vandell took me to the place of Hassan the barber.

Hassan means "horse," but strictly speaking the word means "the most beautiful animal" or just "the most beautiful." It's a proud name not always really suiting those who bear it. In the case of our friend the barber from Blidah, it's easy to believe that his parents so named him on account of the fine opinion he had of himself. Hassan is middle-aged, neither handsome nor ugly, and over-dressed. For an Arab he's too familiar—perhaps it's his trade that makes him that way. He sees and receives all sorts of people. I gather that those who frequent his shop consider it meant for all and use it as a meeting place as if it were a street corner.

As usual there was a crowd. It was something like an at-home in a middle-class household. Men were playing chess and checkers, smoking pipes belonging to the proprietor of the shop (Hassan's pipe rack is the best stocked in the quarter), and the *kaouadji* from the café next door brought coffee—that the men paid for themselves.

As we were entering, a very tall young man with a thin face was finishing a game of checkers. He was saying to his adversary, pushing his last pawn toward him, "If everything we wished for happened, a beggar could become *bey*."

Commenting that this is a well-known proverb, Vandell took him by the hand to introduce him to me: "My dear friend, I present to you the wittiest and most learned man in the three provinces, *taleb* [student] at the *ʒaouïa* [Koranic school] in ——, my friend Ben-Hamida, the 'vaudeville artist.' Together you can chat about Paris," he added, "for he" (indicating me) "lives there and Sid-ben-Hamida has spent time there."

I learned from Sid-ben-Hamida himself that he had been a student at the Collège Saint-Louis. He spent the four or five years of his stay in France studying there. I wasn't to know, and probably never will, the real reason for his French education. There are lives like his in this land of inference where the underpinnings of things are sure to remain well hidden.

"I've forgotten nearly all my French," he said, hunting for his words. "I'll end up not being able to speak it at all."

He has a lively, keen, and playful mind that's singularly inventive, and given the chance, he's full of repartee. That education of his begun in our country appears to have developed in him certain characteristics that are uncommonly rare among the Arabs even of the upper classes. His way of presenting himself is open and of talking, discursive. He uses gestures to express himself, also speaking in a bantering tone. When he looks at you it's always with an irresistible smile. He retained only what he wanted from his attendance at our schools: a love of letters and an impish delight in puns and proverbs. It's because of that light touch that's almost French and that literary elegance that Vandell nicknamed him the "vaudeville actor." He was in Moorish dress, and as he was wearing a wintertime turban, his neck, head, and face were enveloped by a scarf of muslin with little pink polka dots.

The man he'd been playing against was a lowland Arab, who was a little short and heavy, bearded, with a brownish complexion. He was wearing burnoose and *haik* with underneath, as is the case with horsemen, a jacket and vest embroidered in silk. A narrow gray silk cord ending in gold tassels combined with the *khrit* (rope of black camel hair) encircled his head; prayer beads hung from his neck, a couple of amulets being attached to his headdress.

"Take a good look at this man," Vandell said. "He's a swordsman—sometime I'll tell you how he uses his sword when he has the chance."

The gathering also included some townsmen of the middle class who lived in the neighborhood. Half of them were sellers of tobacco and spices and the other elderly, graying men of leisure who spoke in low tones, puffing slowly on their pipes and prudently wrapped up in burnooses for house wear, something like dressing gowns. They wore meticulously folded turbans, vests that were buttoned all the way up, and light tan wool stockings ending at the knee. Their slippers were lined up on the floor by the benches and each had within easy reach either a short pink candle or a painted paper lantern. The last two items served to light their way home for the night was very dark.

I'd like you to understand more or less just what they were talking about for homebodies don't get together at such an hour at the barber's with the sole purpose of gathering in a circle to hold their tongues. Arab conversation resembles all those conversations that are basically idle and in which the uselessness of what is said can be explained only by some contagious itching of the tongue.

Pantomime translates its particular style to better effect than the written word. First of all come the greetings. Recurring at fixed intervals like courtesy refrains, they keep track of the rhythm of discourse by fixing the rests and indicating the continuations. They're made up of courtesy words and phrases about everything, questions about everything, blessings on everything (everything except women, who aren't included as something properly to be interested in). They then discuss happenings of all kinds: circumspect, very local gossip about politics, French goings-on as well as minor items concerning quarter, city, and tribe. Moving on, they recount anecdotes about other worlds including *the* other world. Old farfetched conceptions and preconceptions from all time have kept their ability to move and stir people. Those listening who know them best enjoy a good laugh. Everyone knows these anecdotes by heart, yet everyone in turn makes himself happy in a naive way by hearing or recounting them. All that is combined with much play on words, meant mainly for the ear and relying on assonance, and therefore untranslatable. Maxims, conceits, proverbs are mixed in. In this category the scribe Ben-Hamida provides the genuine flowery literary expression of the primordial Arab genius.

In describing the recent siege that he had witnessed, Vandell relied on the obligatory, colorful onomatopoeia. He reproduced the noise of a cannon with a movement of the lips that imitated it very well. Trying to get across the idea of a pitched battle, he kept repeating over and over again as long as he could the unending "ba-ba-ba's" that ordinarily accompany an Arab's account of any adventure where gunpowder has had much to say. The next topic was the *djerad* (grasshoppers) who, it is said, are swarming in the south, soon to start traveling. Measures have been taken, fatigue duty ordered, battues organized to destroy them. Will they elude them? In that connection, a man who had been in Blidah a long time told all about—as heard from his father, who got it from his father, who had been present, but in person, when already very old —that huge disaster, the invasion of all invasions of 1724–25. He described it as comparable to the ones described in Jewish history. The *djerad* had destroyed everything but above all the vineyards, eating first the shoots and the twigs and ending up by even devouring the stocks. Fire couldn't have been quicker or grimmer. Since that time the vines have been unproductive and the wine of Blidah, which used to be famous, is no more. Millions and millions were destroyed without their number appearing diminished; the sky was darkened, the city choked, and the water in the wells was poisoned by them. People got back at this cursed plague as best they could. They made fritters and jam with the grasshoppers, salted them, used them as fertilizer until finally a strong south wind rose up and carried that army of crazed creatures out to sea to drown.

"Following which, they changed into shrimp and the people of the *fhas* fished for them," added Ben-Hamida, who seemed to be having fun with his country's superstitions.

Thereupon, they moved on to monsters—from the dragon of the Hesperides to the "Niam-Niam," creatures Africa has always been thought to produce.

"Africa is always producing something new," Vandell said, taking his turn at being erudite. And after then citing Aristotle he gave the following commentary taken from Pliny: "The scarcity of water forced the animals to crowd together pell-mell near the few streams. Their young as a consequence took all kinds of strange forms, since the males, whether on purpose or not, had coupled, no distinction being made, with females of whatever species." Hassan the barber opined that what happened was self-evident and the old men agreed with Hassan; Ben-Hamida was alone in not admitting that explanation as the last word in modern science and gave a smile.

Here's a final story. They were discussing Sid-Mustapha-ben Roumi, in other words Commandant X, and his well-known saga with Béchir. The anecdote is like something out of the tales of chivalry. An Arab in burnoose, a Hadjout, was telling it, not of course as a new story since it's part of the common lore but as a tale that a man of his people can never repeat too often. And here it is, even if much abbreviated.

Commandant X came as a very young man to Algiers in about the second year after it was taken. In those days Algiers didn't have a secondary school and a French child's early schooling took place out in the streets with the local children. There he learned a variety of things that you learn without an instructor at that age, among them the language of the country and the pleasures that go with being free. The family, however, decided that wasn't the equal of what is learned at home and so tried to change the situation. The boy didn't like the form the changes took, and not tolerating constraints he left his family and fled. When he reached the Sahel outside Algiers and just as he was about to go down toward the plains, and realizing perhaps the hazards of his enterprise, he met up with two Arabs on horseback. They were setting out on a trip or possibly were looking for plunder.

"Who are you?"

"So and so, son of so and so."

"Where are you going?"

"Ahead."

"Do you want to come with us where the Hadjouts live?"

In that period the Hadjouts were people to be terrified of. The boy bravely answered, "Yes, I do."

One of the marauders put him cross-saddle in front of him and that very evening they took him straight to the tent of Caliph Béchir.

"Here's a hostage," the horsemen said.

"No, he's not—he's a child," said Béchir.

"He'll be mine," Béchir's wife said. She adopted him as fortune's gift, had him circumcised, and named him Mustapha, that is, "he who has been purified."

Mustapha grew up in a tent, became burnt by the sun, and in short order could handle a saber. Reared by expert horsemen, he turned into what he is, a fabulous rider. When he reached fifteen they gave him a horse and arms. One fine day when he was eighteen he became bored with tent life as he had before with being housebound. Fighting was going on everywhere, so he could choose between two countries, the one he was born to or his adoptive one. He opted for the former. He left the *douar*, not at night but in full daylight. He told Béchir, "I'm going," and headed straight to Blidah, where he joined up with the spahis. From Blidah he went to Koleah. He became a soldier, no longer being completely free; yet he was always more Arab than French. Two years later a *razzia* was organized against the Hadjout. A guide was necessary who could lead the column, someone who not only knew the route but knew the country, the language, and above all the habits of the enemy. Mustapha was picked. The battle was engaged and they fought. When the fighting was almost over two horsemen met and exchanged fire with their pistols, then charged each other for a hand-to-hand, the younger with a saber and the older with a lance. Just as the horses were about to meet, the combatants recognized each other:

"Mustapha, it's you!"

"Béchir!"

As the Arabs tell it, Béchir was a hero; he was handsome, intrepid, and always rode magnificent steeds. He halted right in front of the young man, feigning barely to touch the youngster's shoulder so as not to tear his burnoose and tossed his lance to him.

"Take it," he said, "and carry it to General X. Tell him that you took Béchir's lance." Disarmed and empty-handed, he then shifted his bridle and disappeared.

And so the evening ended with a legend of heroes. We parted around ten just as the bugle of the Turkish garrison was sounding curfew. Everyone lighted his lantern, put on his babouches, and raised the hood of his burnoose. We all left together except for the Hadjout man, who stayed at the barber's, where he apparently was going to pass the night. The *salam-aleikoum* and *aleikoum-salam* of leave-taking took place in the street.

"A friend is no small thing," Hamida said, taking my hand and that of Vandell with great warmth, "and a thousand is not too many." On that final proverb spoken in the most amiable way, the young *taleb* of the *ʒaouïa* and former student of the Collège Saint-Louis went his way down the tranquil street humming.

"He's charming but hypocritical," Vandell said once we were alone. "'A sweet-tongued man who would suck the teats of a lioness.'"

"And as for the Arab, the one we left at Hassan's," he went on, "he has on his conscience a bit of mischief that makes him somewhat taciturn for he knows that the law has its eye on him. One evening he was returning to the *douar* with a cousin whom (he said) he had reason to be unhappy with. They were both on horseback and had taken back roads when he let his companion go ahead of him. He took his pistol and shot him in the back. The horse without its rider entered the *douar*. The cadaver was discovered days later when they noticed a great many crows and kites circling above some thickets. It was impossible to spot the wound for the body had been torn to shreds by the birds. They suspected, however, the real truth and interrogated Amar-ben-Arif. Lacking any evidence, the matter went no further. It was a family quarrel caused by jealous spite, I believe. The fact concerning the firing of the pistol is real since Amar-ben-Arif himself told me about it.

"So that you'll know," Vandell added, "here are a few details. The wife has been in Blidah for a month, living there alone with her servant, Assra, the black woman who is celebrating the birth of her child. In that house of hers, which you know, there's just her household and some Jews. Her name is Hawa and her friend's name is Aichouna. The festivities today were for the very first child of Assra, and her husband was the black man who was such a fine dancer, wearing himself out as he expressed his joy at being a father. Did you notice that the baby is not very dark at all? It's a miracle according to that sharp-tongued barber. It seems that the father replied, *'Chouia, chouia, sara negro'* (Be patient, be patient, he will be.) Right now, the father's like a high priest of the dance with that son and rears him like—not a whit more or less—a young Jupiter, to the sound of dancing and clashing shields. We'll return to 'the information office' when we need to, but for now let's be cautious with Hassan. Since Ben-Hamida has given us a taste for proverbs, remember and be guided by this maxim, "There are five steps on the way to becoming wise: hold your tongue, listen, remember, act, take note." That's the wisdom of the Arabs, in other words, politics."

It's ten in the morning, my friend, and in two hours I'll be going to see whether Hawa's apartment resembles Delacroix's admirable painting, *Les Femmes d'Alger*.

YES, MY FRIEND, just like it. It also has charm. But is not more beautiful. In nature itself life is more diverse, there are unexpected details, and the nuances are numberless. There are noises, odors, silence, gestures one after the other, and then the passage of time. In a painting a certain character is determinant, a moment in time is fixed, the choice made is perfection, a scene is set for eternity and is absolute. This is the formula: what should be seen rather than what is, the appearance of truth rather than truth. As far as I know, there is no other reality in the realm of art than a selective truth. There would be no point to being extremely clever and a great painter if one didn't include in a work something that reality does not possess. It's in this that man is more intelligent than the sun, for which I thank God.

Precisely at noon I was knocking on Hawa's door. I could hear within several voices all crying at once, *"Minyou?* (who's there?) while from a room above there was another, easily recognizable voice repeating, *"Ache Koune?"* (Who is it?). There was the sound of shutters closing and the same voice saying, *"Ya Assra, heul el bab!"* (Open the door, Assra!) The black woman came and opened up.

Crossing the courtyard, I noticed four rooms with four Jewish households, women soaping swaddling clothes and lots of children in friendly play around the entrances to the rooms as well as newborns that their mothers rocked in mobile cradles looking like hammocks. On the floor above was an open corridor down which I followed Assra, who dragged her heels over the faience-laid floor, her hips wrapped in a narrow *fouta* of orange and blue cloth, serving as smock. When we got to the entrance to her mistress's room the black servant turned her head slightly toward me making exactly the same gesture as she parted the flowered muslin curtain that you can see in the Delacroix painting.

As I entered I saw Hawa, who had been waiting for me. She was lying on a long, low, and wide couch amid a quantity of small cushions that by their disposition indicated that she used it to sleep on.

"Hello," she said, "have a seat."

I sat down, not beside her but at her feet and not too near so that I could get a good look at her.

In the middle of the room there was a lighted narghile. She held the end of the tube in her fingers, which were covered with rings, watching the trembling threads of smoke that escaped from the opening in the amber mouthpiece. The long tube ringed with brown and gold was wrapped about her slim, nicely sinewed leg that was of the yellow of old ivory. Like Cleopatra's serpent the narghile's tube seemed to press against it. She was motionless and pale, half-smiling; the life that stirred within her peaceful form made her confining bodice rise serenely. There was nothing amiss in her attire and entire appearance for she'd taken exquisite care with her dress and makeup as well as the scent she used. She had about her head blue and black scarves. She was possibly a little less covered than a Moorish woman is in her own home, wearing a blue garment richly worked with gold underneath a blue, sleeveless caftan. Contrary to the fashion current here, a kind of wide gold belt with massive clasp held about her rather slender waist a very flowing *fouta* that was of a scarlet hue. Her dress comprised three colors, but the flaming red wiped out the rest, exaggerating even more by its extreme proximity the dull pallor of her skin. Her eyes were lined with antimony and her hands as well as feet were decorated with henna. The heels reddened with the dye "resembled two oranges."

"What's your name," I asked: *"Ouech-esmek?"*

She took another puff and with a pretty movement handed me the mouthpiece of the narghile whose supple tubing remained entwined around her leg.

"Ouech-entekfi?" (What's it to you?) she said drawing the mouthpiece close to my lips.

"So I'll know whether your name is as sweet as your voice."

"My name is Hawa."

"You are well named," I said, repeating that word light as air, make up of vowels and pronounced in one breath just as you breathe, "for your name signifies 'fresh air and friendship.'"

As the conversation lagged, she asked, "Is it warm outside?"

"Very . . . 'the man who seeks shelter from the sun close to the fire is truly mad.'"

Another pause followed this flirtatious line of poetry. It had made her smile.

You should know, my friend, that aside from "sir," "hello," "good-bye" and "sit down" Hawa doesn't know four syllables in a row of pure French, and so I'm reduced to speaking Arabic, not wishing to use *sabir*, that horrible jargon unworthy of her very special voice, and fearful above all of making her appear ridiculous. I willingly accept the same for myself. From that point on our get-together was so very uneventful I'm having a hard time reporting it to you. I added fuel to the narghile and rolled some cigarettes which she smoked; Assra served us coffee; I walked from the door to the closed blinds on the street side to get a good look at the room. I admired the shelves built into the walls and went back to where Hawa was.

Looped three or four times about her neck like an immense necklace were three of those long strings of orange blossoms that the Jews make. They'd all been picked that morning, and the scent was such that to tolerate it and not get drunk you'd have to be a woman, and an Arab woman at that.

Hawa said, "Take it," as she slowly unwound the perfumed length, tossing it to me as if it were a kind of chain.

That's the way time passed—I'd say an hour or two—until I thought that she was feeling sleepy.

"Not at all," she said.

All the same, she was leaning back, her head half on the cushions. The silence was profound, the air made heavy by the overpowering perfumed smoke. You could hear only the murmuring sighs of the narghile as it ran down. Her eyes closed; I saw a slight shadow fall on her cheeks, which then trembled: it was the night-like shadow of her long eyelashes lighting on her cheeks as if two black butterflies. Hawa was motionless just a minute after she had said, "Not at all." Sleep had already claimed this peaceful creature.

As I crossed the courtyard in leaving the house, one of the Jewish children, the youngest of them, turned his head to one side to spit, which, as you know, is a sign of sovereign loathing.

Blidah, February 28

TODAY I witnessed a terrible sight. The four men were criminals, I was told, and looking at them I had no trouble believing it. They were walking two by two in the thick mud under a driving rain. They wore burnooses and were barefoot, their hands tied behind their backs; they were accompanied by a squad of riflemen who were to execute them. To see that the law was obeyed there were also two line battalions as well as cavalry. Both ahead and behind were crowds of people come to watch the execution. The procession proceeded very slowly; bugles were playing a funeral march. They took the men to the end of the Olive Grove off to the left where there is a hillock rising a few meters above a natural ditch. My awful curiosity followed the crowds accompanying those four wretched men to the doing away of their lives.

The weather was overcast and very cold even though it was noon. They first untied them. When the order was given, each took off his burnoose, folded it, and laid it on the ground at his feet. They were then made to stand on the edge of the ditch six paces from each other facing the mountain. The firing squad took up its position ten steps to their rear. It was made up of forty-eight men, twelve for each condemned man. The infantrymen were deployed in a semicircle around the execution site; two squads of cavalry, swords raised, stood to right and left at the edge of the stream to prevent any escapes. Off toward the west the mountain rose almost straight up, wrapped in snow and providing no exit. A curtain of rain contributed further gloom to the somber scene from which all hope of deliverance had now been removed.

With everything in place, an officer rapidly read off the verdict in French, then in Arabic. I could see those terrible documents, able to count their number and calculate, checking my watch, how much time remained for them to be read, estimating the minutes of grace.

They stood there quietly with unflinching aplomb, feet squarely planted on the ground, imperturbable in the face of their approaching death. They let the left hand hang by their side with the right raised to the level of their forehead, index finger raised toward heaven. This is the mysterious pose an Arab assumes as he accepts his fate, calmly waiting for the last moment.

"Do you know what they're thinking about?" Vandell asked. "They say that what is written is written and if their death has not been determined on high, in spite of all the frightful weaponry, in spite of those forty-eight carbines lined up taking aim at them to fire, they'll live."

Once the reading of the document was over, there were a couple of seconds of silence. I could tell it was all over. One of the condemned men tried to turn his head but didn't have the time. Involuntarily, I closed my eyes and involuntarily the explosion made me open them. I saw the four men leap up in place and like clowns fall flat into the ditch. Then I heard four finishing shots and immediately the bugles signaling departure. Just a squad of soldiers was left on duty by the cadavers, who were supposed to be left as they were until evening when they would be turned over, if claimed, to their families.

The rain fell on them all day long. Toward evening the sky cleared and I could go out again to see what had become of them. There were several Arabs with horses and beasts of burden. The men on guard went off, deciding that the sun was going down. It was then, without any cries or tears as if they were loads of wood, each of the cadavers was hoisted and laid across the back of a mule, then tied so it would keep its balance. Without delay the cavalcade started off, disappearing in the direction of Chiffa. The bodies, once torso and legs were stretched out, exceeded the narrow pack saddles that served as litters. Horribly stiff after having been left there for six cold hours, they never bent as they matched the even steps of the animals. You'd have thought the mules were carrying planks.

Blidah, March

SPRING IS settling in. Here we are in this changing season with the sun already hot. The days are radiant and from time to time there are heavy rains caused by storms but never lasting more than a couple of hours. The wind keeps changing directions, hesitating between its winter and summer positions and at any old time making a complete circle. The thermometer stays in the moderate range with an uncommon low of 15 to 18 degrees centigrade and a maximum of 24 to 25. The snows are beginning to melt. The *oued* is at crest. The small streams that feed it are swollen; and the gardens have brightened up considerably because of the joyous movement of the waters' flow. In the plains there's hardly any water; the lake there has pretty much returned to its bed. You can see it to the left of the Mazafran and behind the territory of the Hadjout, stretched out at the feet of the "Tomb of the Christian Woman" along a thin line, which has the shape and scintillating brilliance of a long sword.

Sometimes, following a week of steady heat, the sky is shrouded with vapors and the atmosphere, particularly above the city, is so dense, hanging so low that the mountain disappears, being half-hidden in a bizarre way as if a stage behind a closing curtain. Even though it abuts us, we now can make out only its base and the reaches of the wooded ravines which impenetrable shade have made dark blue. If the wind remains soft and the fog instead of decomposing into dew rises to where the clouds usually are, it's almost certain we'll hear toward evening one or two thunderclaps from the direction of the mountain. We will then see rain fall, continuing on till morning. At about four, however, we can make out the stars. The bad weather dissipates during the night; as if chased away by the coming day, the clouds vanish helter-skelter along with the shadows. The sun reappears in the sky and not the least bit of perturbation remains; the skyline is distinct, well-defined, solid. We're able to count the cedars that have been planted at three thousand feet above our heads on the highest slopes of the Beni-Salah.

Usually, the evenings are magnificent and I spend them in the Olive Grove. At this time of year (March 12) the sun sets a little after six right where the plains begin, between the first promontory of the Mouzaia and the mountainous terrain of the Beni-Menasser, which resembles some rough sea. You can see the sun suspended like a globe above that high violet barrier, or where there are clouds, presenting a shining triangle of flame. As it goes down, the orb grows larger and just for a moment, since it's not emitting heat or rays, you can look at it without strain. Finally, it plunges among the hills, all red and as if torn apart by the sharp edges of the horizon, and disappears. Right off, a glowing twilight takes over, lasting just a few minutes. Dampness comes before night falls, and less than a quarter hour after the sun's departure, the entire countryside is bathed in dew.

I hardly ever go the Olive Grove except to watch this spectacle, one of the most beautiful a day can offer. It used to be a place we liked for all sorts of reasons, but in any case some of these no longer exist. Perhaps it's lost some of its attractiveness—perhaps also we were younger then. We'd linger in the shade stretched out on the grass, leaning back on the trunk of a tree to discuss all the usual memories. We would watch the small wild olives that were dropping around us as the spring breeze shook the branches of the trees. At such a moment we were still capable of dreaming of matters both grave and great, there in the shadow of those age-laden trees in front of the small marabout with its low dome rather resembling an altar. I remember our reading *Oedipus at Colonus* in that spot an afternoon that recalled Greece. "Stranger, you are now in the loveliest spot in Attica, Colonus, which is rich in swift horses. . . . In this place beneath the heaven-sent dew the flowers of the narcissus with their graceful calix, crown of the ancient goddesses, bloom each day. In this land there grows a tree that neither Asia nor the great Dorian Isle of Pelops can claim, a tree that was not planted by mortal hand, that exists without needing care, that enemy lances back off from. In no other place does it grow so vigorously as in this land. This is the pale-leafed olive tree."

Men clad in white, with a look of seriousness, would stroll under the trees a ways off. We were cut off from the city whose white towers we could see through thorny hedges of prickly pears and aloes. Some horsemen ("tamers of steeds") were making their way over the narrow road between the mountain and where we were, we who were half-naked, without saddles, riding a pair of small horses with restless jaws and short ears in whom we detected a Thessalian look.

The "sacred wood" of Blidah today is no longer recognizable. Everything is going to ruin. The pale-leafed olive trees are losing their crowns of foliage; and the trembling greenery at the end of the branches is so meager and miserable you can longer find any shade at their feet. "Enemy lances" did not "back off from them," and neither Jupiter, protector of the sacred olive trees nor Minerva of the blue eyes will prevent the hands of strangers from uprooting them.

The Arabs haven't held the market here in a long time even though there's no spot for one in Blidah as picturesque as this. Now you can see huts, and most of the time military encampments as well as ditches acting as water conduits, help for the dying trees that's been too long delayed. Only the marabout survives, still lit from within by a quantity of pink candles and small lamps, still giving off, as if a chapel, a warm, mysterious odor of wax that's being consumed, plus incense. It will last as long as superstition does, meaning longer most probably than the olive trees.

There's pleasant news that I haven't shared with you: the storks are back. The other day I saw their emissary. It was early in the morning when many people in Blidah were still asleep. He was coming from the south, borne by a light wind, working his large black-tipped wings that hardly moved, his body suspended between them "as if between two flags." A flock of doves, ravens and small kites were making a joyous fuss around him, welcoming him with squawks and the beating of wings. Eagles were flying a distance away, their eyes turned toward the rising sun. I then saw the stork with escort in tow come down from the mountain and head off in the direction of Bab-el-Sebt.

There were some Arabs around who no doubt had traveled all night for they were lying every which way among their exhausted dromedaries whose loads were piled together in the center of the encampment, only saddle packs being left with the beasts themselves. When the sacred bird passed over their heads, one of the Arabs who saw it stretched out his arm, saying as he stood up, *"Chouf el bel-ardi!"* (Look, there's the stork!). Then all of them glimpsed it and, as if it were someone who had just come back from a trip, looked at it, commenting to each other, *"Chouft' ouchi?"* (Did you see it?) The bird appeared to hesitate for a long time, at first almost brushing against walls, then rising to a great height, feet extended behind him, turning his head slowly in every direction in this, his rediscovered country. At one point he looked to want to land but the wind that had carried him here pulled his wings back, carrying him off to where the lake is.

The storks emigrate in autumn and return in the spring. They rarely show up in the lowlands and never make their home in Algiers. But in Médéah on the contrary and in all the mountain villages they gather in great numbers; Constantine is full of them. To my knowledge there are few houses in this city, which is the most African and the least Oriental of all Algerian cities, as well as few roofs of any real height that don't have a nest. Each mosque has its own; sometimes there are several. It's beneficial for a house to have been chosen by the storks for like the swallows they bring good luck to their hosts. There's a whole legend that makes them sacred creatures to be protected: they are *tolbas* who have been changed into birds after having eaten during the fast. They reassume human form every year in some unknown country that's far away. When they balance on just one leg, throwing their heads around to the rear, and with a snapping of their beaks make the singular sound of "kwam, kwam, kwam," it's at that moment that the *tolba*'s soul, which is still alive within them, is beginning its prayers. Once it was Antigone, the daughter of Laomedon and Priam's sister, whom Juno changed into a stork to punish her for pride brought on by her beauty. Each nation has a knack for metamorphosing things and each puts its own history into it: the Greek, who was artistic, had to be punished for female vanity; the Arab, who is devout but gluttonous, is punished for a sin committed during the time of fasting.

Blidah, March

TODAY WE made a trip down into the ravine of Oued-el-Kébir. Oued-el-Kébir in spite of the attribute "big" is a very small river indeed—in France we'd call it a stream—that with winter rains and melting snows can all of a sudden become a torrent. Reduced to its own resources it's nothing. It rises from the bottom of a narrow ravine and isn't very deep. As with all mountain streams if first you come across it at its source, it's nicely cradled among rocks, decked out with shrubs, reeds, and oleander. There quite removed, among cool shadows and in silence, it's born like an idea from the peaceful thoughts of some solitary man.

Only a few years ago whenever they undertook this little trip of at most two kilometers from their city the people in Blidah wouldn't leave their houses without a loaded gun on their shoulder.

They believed it wise to be more than one and each armed. Today, of course, everyone goes alone to the headwaters of the Oued smoking his cigar and with a great sense of security, and more pleasantly, too. It's as if they're off to the public gardens of the Tapis-Vert.

Just at the entrance to the gorge they've built mills and what will be factories, I believe, for bricks. A short way from there they're constructing a dam that will stabilize the stream's flow. Consequently, it's only a hundred meters farther on that the walk becomes interesting. The path ventures into the ravine between its steep, very picturesque flanks among boulders fallen from the mountain rolled about by the stream when in flood. The Oued runs to one side of the path over a bed of sand or gravel that resembles powdered slate. At times the bed has large rocks that the current goes around, foaming a bit, its strength insufficient to wrench them out. The mountain is rocky, jagged, and in many places marked by deep landslides. You don't see many trees. Every once in a while there are some old olive trees that have taken root almost horizontally in the mountainside, holding on with their roots, their disheveled branches hanging over the path. A little farther on the gorge widens and divides up into lateral ravines. The vegetation grows lusher. And where the mountain has ceded a place ground pools fed from below have formed, encumbered by greenery.

We're nearing the cemetery, which is as you saw it, closed in with rustic fences made of dead trees and brushwood and further protected by an impenetrable belt of lentisk, myrtle, and vines. It's deep within a shaded wood of big, very green olive trees, carob that are even more somber, immense ash trees, and aspen with their whitish trunks and the size and look of plane trees. Quite alone and sheltered in the middle of these lonely surroundings, where the sun only enters at midday, is a plot crowded with plants and tombs. Only three or four of the tombs have the monuments common to marabouts. These are about four or five feet high with

Blidah

105

a sawtooth crown, the *kouba* shaped like a cone. Such is the common sepulcher of religious figures or those with some other distinction.

An old woman was guarding the cemetery. She squatted on the ledge of a tomb with her head on her knees. She wore a smock striped with blue, bright yellow, and brilliant red that was poorly secured at the shoulders. Her arms and feet were uncovered, her head wrapped in a black scarf, her face half-hidden by hair that was completely gray. She held in her hands like an emblem of all human frailty a long, thin reed wand.

"Greetings to you, oh Mother! May your day go well!" was Vandell's opening.

"What is it? What do you wish?" the old woman asked, a bit alarmed on seeing us all of a sudden in the restricted area. We answered, "We only wish well," and sat on a section of fence.

A pink candle was burning in the hollow of a toppled tree in the middle of the cemetery. The fronts of the four marabouts, which all faced east, were coated with melted wax. In a sort of niche in the wall of the most ornate as well as the oldest of the four another fragrant wick was burning, though we could see only its smoke.

"'Do you know who those people were, you who know everything?" I asked Vandell.

"They were men," was the rather pompous answer. "If you really want, I can tell you their names and their legends, which is more appropriate than 'their histories,' but what's the point? They had their day; they lived in a country that's not yours and spoke a language which you hardly understand. If they did good or evil, it's of no concern to you; and we don't even have the right to light a pink candle in their honor."

As we were leaving by the gate, an Arab who had just entered the enclosure went to kiss the tomb of the saint with great devotion, then since it was about one in the afternoon, went down on his knees to recite the third prayer.

A village lies hidden a few steps back from the cemetery. It's where the old aristocracy of Blidah used to stay. Pillaged, then burned in 1836, pillaged again in 1840, today it's reduced to around fifteen structures, of which only one has a tile roof, all the others being covered with reeds. Dogs were on guard at the entrance. They barked at our heels while children bawled as if there were some new siege.

We kept on with our walk, talking about death most philosophically.

"I don't believe in it," my companion said. "It's a dark passage that each of us encounters at a given moment in his life, and it alarms many people, specifically those whom the darkness frightened when they were children. In my case, the three or four times that I happened to find myself quite close to it, I saw on the other side a little light, what kind exactly I don't know, but quite clear, and it calmed me down completely."

April

I'VE SEEN Hawa often in the past three weeks and we are now most definitely good friends. It had been clear in any case from the beginning that we wouldn't have much difficulty in becoming such. Vandell, who tends to go along with everything I propose, usually accompanies me on my visits and we light the narghile in his honor. As interpreter that's his right, and since the narghile has three extensions and we all have use of a tube, our conversation often consists of each of us in turn making the rose-perfumed water murmur in its crystal container. That's how we spend the warm afternoons, or sometimes evenings, indolently reclining on cushions. I have complete freedom to poke about in Hawa's cupboards and chests and do so. I open up the great chests the color of cinnabar with their copper locks, out of which I'll sometimes take her clothes or maybe her jewelry. She has one of the richest and most varied Arab-style wardrobes: jackets for summer and for winter; little vests all covered with work in gold with enormous gold or silver buttons; cotton or silk caftans; pantaloons for the leisure hours which are fairly plain and of the simplest of cotton stuff or Indian muslin and for dress in heavy brocade bedizened with silk and gold; plus an assortment of *foutas;* gauzy scarves to be worn with turbans; pieces of cloth serving as head coverings or belts. All these items with their terribly clashing colors have bizarre names that it would be useless to repeat. The jewelry is kept separately, wrapped in a scarf. There are bangles for the legs; bracelets; chain bracelets made up of coins; hand mirrors with handles inlaid with mother-of-pearl; slippers, too, are represented for by their air of luxury as well as cost they are genuine pieces of jewelry.

"You must have been in the will of a sultan," I said to Hawa the day that I discovered that fine chest with its wealth of things for an elegant woman.

"No sultan gave me that, it was my husband."

"Which one," Vandell interrupted, unaware that his joke would hit the mark so squarely.

"The one who died," Hawa answered with a degree of sadness in her voice convincing us that she had been widowed.

"And what did you do with your second husband?" I asked.

She hesitated at first, then grew pale—as pale as a face can become that never has a hint of color—and looking straight at us in turn, answered, "I left him."

"You did the right thing after all if he bored you" was Vandell's way of concluding the matter.

That same evening Vandell went to Hassan's to get some more information. He learned that in fact Hawa had lost her first husband and had been divorced from her second after six months of marriage. Hassan did not, however, say more. I don't know why, but he seemed set on not naming either of the two persons responsible for first Hawa's fortune and second her misfortune. Hawa is an Arab. She was born in the lowlands. If the information is correct, her father belonged to the Arib, a family with Saharan origins who settled in the Mitidja without legal permission. They lived there scattered among the tribes and preying on them all up until 1834 when the French administration grouped them together as an auxiliary force, a sort of advance lookout. Hawa then still has a little Saharan blood in her veins and her tawnier complexion, her darker or more fiery eyes, the singularly adolescent look of her body that hasn't taken on the chubbiness common with Moorish women, suitably match her origins. We supposed that she must belong through marriage either to the Beni-Khrelil or, more likely, to the Hadjout. Nonetheless, this supplementary information is of concern for vital statistics—if such exist among the Arabs—and not needed by us. Since that time, what was revealed to us by chance about Hawa's history was never mentioned again. As for her divorce we knew only that it meant she was free and thus the attentions of her two new friends could rightfully cause no one to take umbrage.

While the house is very noisy on the ground floor, above all whenever there's a neighborly dispute among the Jewish women, upstairs where the taciturn Hawa lives alone in the front gallery rooms that she shares with Assra and her husband, who spends the night there, it couldn't be quieter. We can find her there at no matter what time of day, except when it's the hour for the baths, in a dark corner of the room where she sits or reclines on her divan, making up her eyes, playing with her mirror, smoking her water pipe. She's decked with chains of flowers like a madonna and her arms are cold as marble; her splendid eyes seem vague and inert as if exhausted by the deadly inactivity of the life she leads without anyone about, either family or children. She's a singular example of an almost perfect beauty who's alive yet sterile—if you can call it being alive. Who knows what incomprehensible destiny seems to prevent her from being a wife and condemns her never to be a mother. The pull she exerts is strange as well: it's very strong yet superficial, not going I would imagine deeper than the heart's outer layer. She has a woman's seductive ways without the will or plain desire to seduce. You listen to her, contemplate and admire her, and are captivated by something that's charming without being drawn to it. She is a kind of bizarre creation that would be monstrous in Europe, where a woman is a woman. Just imagine something like an exotic flower that's both exquisite and rare, born for an Oriental gynaeceum. During the period of youthful bloom it beautifies and perfumes the dwelling, comparable, if you will, to the most subtle of perfumes whose enchantment is wafted unbeknownst to the same useless, delightful being.

One day, like today, when I was hunting for things to compare her to, my friend Vandell remarked, "You talk about a kind of flower but you've yet to find the word that fits. All such terms are too active to impart the idea of that embryonic existence that knows neither initiative nor consciousness. You need a neutral verb, and the more neutral the better. I propose a Latin one: *olet* [she exhales]. Tack on an adjective to indicate the attraction of this fragrant effluvium: you could say that she smells good—radiating like a good scent. I think that's all you can really say about her, and as far as we're concerned, we're just sensual creatures whom the nearness of an exotic plant pleasantly provides with perfume. There's nothing very dangerous in all this as long as we get a breath of fresh air from time to time. And yet it makes you question the human soul."

Hawa's voice is music, as I told you the day when I'd heard her for first time; it's music rather than speech. She speaks rather the way birds sing. In addition, you must appreciate mysterious melodies and listen as you would to the sound of the wind in order to enjoy conversations with Hawa. When you wish to increase the tenderness of tone, you have to call her *aïni* (my eye). She'll then respond with *habibi* (my friend) or sometimes *ro'ahdiali* (my soul). Nothing is more musical and less passionate: her speech is like, say, a nightingale singing in its cage. I'm really hard put to tell you what we do in her company or how we pass the time. We go in, we stay a bit, and we leave her, today's memories being not more acute or more memorable than those of the day before. All the while, the sun is going down over the courtyard, lighting the room. A fine dusting of gold filters through the thin cloth of the curtain hung across the doorway. This illumination lasts only a moment, and during it the entire, constricted interior full of silk cloth, inlaid furniture, lighted cabinets, and decorated porcelain is invaded by fiery reflections. Once the sun has gone down behind the terrace twilight enters the room. Colors then vanish and the golds are extinguished, the narghile gives off bluer smoke, and we become aware of the fire in its base. Evening is not far away; thus we reach day's end.

On occasion we've had supper with Hawa. On those days the afternoons are spent in the kitchen pounding black pepper, cinnamon, and saffron in a mortar as well as kneading *couscoussou,* then simmering it on a low fire. Assra takes care of the honeyed pastries. Vandell, who vaunts, and with reason, having been dined by the Caliphs of all three provinces introduces dishes of an almost fabulous nature to Hawa's table. Invariably, the base in all that princely cuisine is small pieces of meat and a great quantity of dried fruit; the novelty depends, however, on the choice, abundance, and aggressiveness of the spices.

When by chance Hawa's great friend, the beautiful, white-skinned Aichouna, arrives at the dinner hour, or what's more polite, has her little black maid Yasmina announce that morning that she'll be coming, the party is complete for we can be assured that there'll be competition between the two friends as to both dress and makeup. We were given that pleasure the other night. Aichouna came at around six. She was accompanied by her servant dressed all in red. As she entered the room she removed her large veil, and dropping her black leather sandals at the carpet's edge, came and reclined on the divan in all her magnificence, like an idol. She was quite wonderful with her legs twisted about a *fouta* gathered below her waist, a bodice decorated with pieces of metal as if a dagger's sheath and a simple blouse of silver-starred gauze that—with quite comprehensible vanity—had as its only purpose to dot the almost total nudity of her shoulders and bust with gleaming accents.

"She might as well not be wearing anything underneath," commented Vandell as he saw her enter, "for what's there is so sheer it could easily be vapor."

"My dear friend, don't you know that those decorous admirers of transparency, the Indians say? They compare those sheer chiffons to running water." Our beautiful Aichouna agrees with them, dressing herself in a metaphor.

Then Hawa, who had absented herself for an hour, parted the curtain of her dressing alcove to appear before us. She was wearing with a great air the imperial dress of a woman from Constantine, that is, three long caftans, one over the next. Two were of flowered muslin while the third, which was of cloth of gold falling without folds, lent a certain stiffness to her supple carriage, enclosing her in a sort of spectacular armor. A scarf, also of cloth of gold and twisted in a bizarre way, completely concealed her hair, resting like an Oriental mitre over the uplifted arc of her painted eyebrows. She wore few jewels and no rings, a bit of modesty that seemed in perfect taste. A line of antimony lengthened her superb eyes, narrowing them a bit, causing them to smile involuntarily. A tiny star in pale-blue paint marked the middle of her forehead with a hieratic, mysterious symbol. She entered, moving without lifting her bare feet from the thick wool carpet; she opened a Turkish handkerchief saturated with perfume, releasing the scent. She drew near the very low divan and placed her brown, fluttering hand on the bare shoulder of her friend. Instead of sitting, she let herself slide down with a movement of indescribable lassitude.

"Marvelous!" Vandell proclaimed as he greeted her with the ceremony due a queen.

Lying on our sides we dined on the carpet around a small marquetry table with candles resting on a tablecloth made of a black woman's *haik;* there the dishes were served. We were waited on by two black women, and for the occasion it was Assra's husband who poured from the ewer and handed us the colored silk napkin.

After dinner, which lasted a long time, we took coffee followed by tea, smoking without interruption until ten o'clock. Aichouna was the first to get up. She wrapped around her the thick *haik* that's the fashion in Blidah yet more negligently than she would have in broad daylight. Part of it was folded twice about her head, the rest falling around her like a coat. With her height, her gleaming silver bodice, her partially exposed bosom, and the rather grandiose effect of that floating drapery, I found her more imposing than without a veil. My eyes followed her to the end of the veranda as she walked noiselessly in the moon's milky light. Yasmina, who carried something heavy wrapped in a corner of her blood-red *haik*, followed her.

Laughing, Vandell commented, "It's only pastries, you know."

A storm happened to break out as we were having our coffee. The rain came down hard, and it was so dark it would have been impossible to find our way without groping at walls. In such weather a lamp would have been completely useless. And so I asked Hawa whether she would allow us to spend the night at her place. She graciously agreed.

"Don't worry about us," I told her. "Si-bou-Djâba will 'work on his maps,' I'll write or sleep when so inclined. Good night, and see you in the morning."

"Good night to both of you," she said.

She went and stretched out on the divan that served as her bed. It's a sort of masonry platform covered and backed with glazed tile. There were three or four layers of *djerbi*, a mattress of quilted silk, cushions for the body, and satin pillows to support the head. Following the Arab custom, Hawa lay down completely dressed and shortly was asleep.

There was no movement either in the street or in the house.

The Jews on the ground floor had shut themselves in early in the evening, having no other means to prevent water from entering than to barricade themselves, closing the sole aperture, stuffing its corners. The children no longer shouted. The whole night was filled with the continuous pouring down of the rain that bounced off the terraces to fall on the courtyard that now looked like a pool. I went downstairs to secure the outside door that had only been pushed shut. I put in place the crosspiece. As I passed in front of the room where Asra lay near her husband, I heard him snoring like a sleeping lion. She was softly humming an African air to coax her child to sleep.

Vandell had changed the candles and having undone the documents in longhand that he always carries about, in this particular case two or three rolls from his pockets, began plotting the itinerary of his upcoming trips. He lent me his notebook that reminded you a bit of hieroglyphs—like the man himself. As well as I could, I read about his recent excursion to the south in the eastern region of the Algerian Sahara. Thus we spent that rainy night: he planning fresh adventures and I reflecting on the little I'd seen, not daring to dream about expeditions that are outside my ken.

I'm not a traveler, my friend, as I've told you more than once. I am at most a wanderer. If I were to undertake an expedition, my contribution wouldn't even be to rouse the curiosity of others to follow in my footsteps. In vain I'd travel all the roads of the world and geography, history, or science wouldn't benefit from a fresh piece of information. What I remember about things is often not worth the telling, for even if quite accurate, it never carries the solidity of a document acceptable to all. In any case, the weaker a recollection becomes, the more it's transformed, becoming my memory's thing, the better it is for what I do, wrongly or rightly, with it. As the exact form of the recollection alters, it becomes something else, half real and half imaginary, and which I find preferable. All that doesn't make for a traveler; to operate in this way proves on the contrary that I wasn't born to go long distances.

"Have you seen Sid-Okaba?" Vandell asked as he followed on his map the dotted line going from Biskra to Oued-Ghrir.

I told him I had on my second trip.

"Do you remember the mosque and the sepulcher of that holy man, the vicar of the Prophet as well as one of his first lieutenants? Did you notice the special shape of the monument, which is one of the most curious in the hills of Zab? And did they relate to you the famous legend attached to it?"

Seeing that I was embarrassed to answer, he said, "So what did you do at Sidi-Okba if you don't even know about it the one thing there is to know?"

"My dear friend," I told him, "the day I passed that way it was fine but very hot. The white-hot sky hung like a polished tin mirror above the village that was half wiped away after a half-day of sun and no clouds. They took me to see the mosque and I saw it; they told me its history and I listened. But what I remember clearly is what followed. They had prepared a collation for us in a garden. They were mats on the ground at the foot of a fig tree and over our heads some tent cloth forming a triangle attached by ropes to three palm trees. The caid, whose picture I could paint for you, served us. Our horses were tethered in the same enclosure, their nostrils inflamed and their mouths foaming from the morning's ride. It was noon, it being—I'll give you the exact date—March 15, 1848. We had left the smala of a nephew of Sheik El-Arab, a Ben-Ganah, rich and handsome as are all the members of that magnificent clan. We were on the road, by then more or less halfway from the *douar* to the village, and an Arab messenger had been looking for us since morning. He hurried toward us riding hard. He was supposed, he said, to deliver to us on behalf of the commandant a communication as well as the front page of a newspaper. The letter and the newspaper that said above the masthead, 'French Republic' informed us of unexpected and very important news,[17] as you will see. In that very garden in the midst of a circle of people not one of whom spoke my language, and very suspicious as are the Arabs, I reread one and the other with great care after the meal. You're aware how news gets about in this country —carried by the wind. The palm trees as their fronds rubbed together made a certain sound as if forebodings had a tongue. The circumstance and the place caused me to pick some of those spotted palm leaves. I thought of my friends in France. A rifle shot made hundreds of sparrows and doves sleeping in the hollow of trees take flight. I remember that as I saw all the suddenly wakened birds precipitously taking off, I thought that my own tranquillity of mind was fleeing with them. That's what I've left of my visit to Sid-Okba: the date of a politically unsettling moment mixed all of a sudden with an African pastoral along with a bunch of palm fronds fixing my memories for all time."

"A nice outing," was Vandell's comment. He hadn't listened to the first word of my story and for the hundredth time since I've known him the traveler who was born to travel had judged the artist.

The rain halted sometime between five and six and you could hear the roosters, who had been silent since midnight, begin to crow. Animals housed in a neighboring *fondouk* began to stir in the straw, making early morning noises over their empty feeding troughs. The moon was rising. It was in its last quarter, its disk turned all the way upside down, a sign, they say, of a coming storm, and too feeble to light the night; it resembled a broken ring. Hawa had never broken her sleep for a minute. Absolutely nothing at all in her dress was disturbed, but the orange flowers that she likes to adorn herself with both day and night had wilted from the warmth of sleep. Their odor too had much diminished so that you could hardly smell them. As I gazed at her covered with her favorite flowers—those dying flowers—sleeping a dreamless sleep, sunk in rest as deep as forgetting, a bitter thought—I don't know why—occurred to me, making me comment to Vandell, "Isn't it a bad sign when flowers around a woman's neck wilt quickly?"

But the sum of Vandell's reply was to gesture for my benefit toward the eastern sky where dawn was breaking.

"You're right," he said, "daylight mustn't overtake us enjoying our good luck. Let's get moving."

We exited cautiously as if afraid to displease the chaste eyes of the newborn day.

3

Mustapha d'Alger

Mustapha d'Alger, April

I'M WRITING TO YOU from Algiers, where I've come to take part in the "feast of the fava beans" (Aïd-el-Fould). It's a holiday of the blacks. They celebrate it every year during the month of April when the first fava beans are harvested. Why fava beans in particular? What is the religious meaning of the feast day? Why this bull dressed in fine cloth, adorned with bouquets of flowers, and which a sacrificing executioner kills by slitting its throat as part of a barbaric ceremony? Why a fountain, the lustral water, and the bull's blood with which the crowd gets sprinkled as if by sacred rain? Why is it that it's specifically women who carry it out and for whom it exists? A woman distributes the blood and is the first one to take water from the fountain, and if the men perform the dances it's women who seem to be in charge. There are a number of points concerning the Aïd-el-Fould of Algiers that are explained in different books, but let me confine myself to telling what I saw. The picture presented is most unusual and quite spectacular. Not once did I think today that this completely African ceremony, which is a mixture of tragic pomp plus amusements, dancing, and feasting, was anything other that a big show conceived by this joyous group of people to dazzle each other and have a great good time. Once a year they allow themselves the combined pleasures of great display, sanctioned gaiety as well as intemperate behavior.

The feast takes place by the sea between the military training ground and the hamlet of Husein-Dey around a sacred tomb. This lies deep among the cactus on a large esplanade where the view is both of the limitless sea and the Hamma. The elevated site could not be better chosen as such a vast stage set where two or three thousand spectators gather for the feast, all of them blacks, both men and women. Tents are put up, makeshift ovens are built, kitchens open to the breeze are organized—more or less like our country fairs. Moorish cooks gather with all their pots and pans, and as soon as the ceremony is over meals are served, which is definitely the most serious occupation that day. Below that amphitheater ringed with tents and decorated with flags, down on the beach itself is the other half of the crowd. They're the fanatics who are in charge of the ceremony, the faithful who want to follow it from close up and those curious Europeans or Arabs who've come to see. Finally, there are those several hundred blacks having hastened there with the determination, courage, and vigor to dance twelve hours without stopping, which, let it be said, is a superhuman tour de force.

When the procession arrived it was hard to find a place to see, and I only glimpsed the bull. Although it was far away and the sea dulled its effect, I heard a horrible music of iron crotals, drums, and hautboys that erupted on to the beach, announcing the arrival of the cortege. The crowd immediately pressed forward, and I could gather from the concentric circle it formed that the bull must be in the center. A few minutes later the circle opened so that you could see the victim stretched out on the sand with its throat cut and in the process of spilling its remaining blood. As soon as it had been struck down, the more excited threw themselves at it and the instant it had finished bleeding started to cut it up. The act of butchering it took place at the foot of the shrine and as near as possible to the fountain so that the lustrations and the sacrifice could take place at the same moment. Many of the spectators then went down to the spring, and for a good part of the morning I could see small bottles of water being passed up. Looking satisfied, the black women came back from there with blood splattered on their faces, the scarlet of the blood disappearing in the purple color of their *haiks*—a detail worth noting.

Just imagine a thousand women at least, which is more than half of that strange assembly. From their dress they can't be told one from the other since the standard shrouding veil hides the numberless splendors of color. Every woman is wrapped in red, a fierce red without any nuance or softening admixture, the pure red that a painter's palette can scarcely reproduce, made fierier yet by the sun. It achieves an ardent extreme with the help of other exacerbating sensations. Indeed, this vast display of flame-colored fabric was spread out over the spring's grassy carpet, which was the most vivid green. It was further set off by the sea, which was the strongest of blues for there was little wind and the water merely rippled. From a distance what you saw at first was a grassy knoll haphazardly dotted with poppies. Close up, the effect of those singular flowers became unbearable. When a dozen of these women were grouped along with their children dressed just like their mothers they created a solid mass of vermilion. It was impossible to face such dazzle without being practically blinded. Everything paled next to this inimitable red. Its violence would have terrified Rubens, the only one whom red of whatever kind never frightened. This was his dominant note forcing other colors to blend in gentle harmonies.

The black population of Algiers had emptied its chests and drawers, holding back nothing as it retrieved with the excessive ostentation of the poor, the greedy, and the uncivilized apparel of unexpected opulence plus accessories and jewelry. These were the wardrobes of the women breadsellers and of servants, who hide treasures no one is aware of. All is in keeping to be shown on just that special holiday. Like ships hoisting their flags, they had decked themselves with the richest things they owned, or rather what was most bizarre and arresting. Not one of them wore the common blue veil. Sad-colored checkered *haiks* served as tablecloths for those who had none other or to make tents, shelters, or parasols: shaded by their servant attire these slaves disguised as princesses enjoy a day of independence in luxury.

You saw the product of Oriental dyeing skills which is both vivid and, combined with what the polychrome tastes of black people can imagine, unusual. There were silks, multicolored wool things, little blouses in lamé, striped, dotted, with needlework spangles and whose sleeves billowed and sparkled; little bodices in cloth, others covered with bits of metal, fastened high up so as to constrict the bosom, magnifying it. *Foutas* of fine crinkly silk of all imaginable colors clothed the lower extremities of the women like so many mutable rainbows. A great variety of jewelry was distributed in profusion over cloth and flesh: much gilt, glass beads, pearls, coins, coral, necklaces of shells from the Guinea Coast, flacons of perfume brought from Istanbul, leg bangles called *khrot-krahl* because of the noise they make knocking together as a woman walks. Everywhere goldsmiths' handiwork glittered on black bosoms. Imagine even three or four pendants on the same ear; mirrors in turbans; bracelets one after the other from wrist to elbow; rings on all fingers; and of course flowers. So many hands were busy manipulating handkerchiefs as if fans and from a distance they resembled white birds taking flight.

When you see these black women in their day-to-day lives dressed in somber blue, conducting their small businesses on street corners, their attire is as drab as their manner is taciturn. It would be hard to foresee what these people who are so fond of joyful noise can become once they have dressed up and come to life. They then assume their natural ways for they are sprightly and keen. Warmth excites them and the sun, which is kind to them, suits them as it does reptiles. They're a strange group of people, unsettling to

Mustapha d'Alger

contemplate—like a sphinx that won't stop laughing—full of contrasts and contradictions. From being in a state of nature and free like animals they were transported all over the world, acclimatized, subjugated, and I was about to say—may mankind forgive me—domesticated like animals. They were both robust and docile, patient even when chained, bearing with ingenuity an abominable fate.

They have caressing eyes, a lisping voice, and a gentle way of speaking. Being both beautiful and repellent, their faces are as funerary as night's own, and yet they are jovial. When they smile it's with a gaping mouth like a classical mask, thus providing something strangely misshapen to precisely what's most pleasing in a face's expression.

They are comical even when serious and laughable as well as being full of laughter. These poor people's most authentic characteristic is joy. I saw in a few hours more white teeth and open lips than I'll see in a lifetime in our European world, where the outlook is less philosophical. All sorts were represented there and the beautiful women were very varied—some almost perfect—and for the most part all were most original in their presentation and manner. That can beautify ugliness itself. (I'm talking to you here about women since in this picture men are way in the background.) Their veils framed their faces without covering them and descended no further than the waist. On their feet as long as the religious feast lasted, they were massed on the slopes and crammed together in compact groups as if human terraces. Every outcropping held a group. During part of the afternoon the ruins of an old brick wall served as a pedestal for an assembly of statues, perhaps the most beautiful young women of the feast.

They were tall with straight noses, shining eyes, and cheeks as firm and smooth as basalt. Their hair was done in the Egyptian style and their contours were so healthy and strong that in spite of the generous nature of the veils and the *foutas*, their muscles, as if under a wet sheet, appeared so very clearly alive. They made up an unbroken line facing the empty horizon, standing out against the blue enamel of the sea with the concreteness of a Chinese painting. Four or five of them were dressed in red; there was one in the center dressed in green, and she was thin, long of limb, supple as a reed by a riverbank, and very pretty with her black turban and bits of silver on her deep red bodice. They held each about the waist, their fingers interlaced, linked to each other by beautiful arms with fine wrists. Their heads were held high, bosoms projecting, hips a trifle misshapen by their habit of squatting most of the time, and feet meeting like those of so many Isises. Some others who were stretched out prone on the grass lay with their chests pressing the ground in a languorous way that was a bit animal-like for they were made to look as if they were crawling. Some others instead, who were off to one side, chatted among themselves, busying themselves with their toilets, arranging acacia blooms next to their cheeks out of that paradoxical liking for what will precisely make them appear even blacker.

An undefinable murmuring, a wordless babbling that filled the air with its slight noise, also added to the very singular effect produced by that army of dark-skinned women. You would have thought it was a tribe of Ethiopian amazons or the harem of some fabulous sultan surprised on an afternoon of merrymaking. It was most beautiful. Following, however, that coming together of costuming and statuary, of pure form and barbaric fantasy, a display of detestable taste—yet all the same overpowering—was to follow. Besides, let's not talk about taste where such a subject is concerned. Let's leave the rules aside for today. We are dealing with a picture without any real organization, having almost nothing to do with art. Let's be realistic now and refrain from judging, as I did when I walked about, looking, noting details, living only through my eyes, having plunged without any reservations or qualms into that whirlwind of colors in movement.

The setting for this picture, as I said, was an amphitheater, and its surroundings were as beautiful as they were vast: a terrain covered with plants and tall grass without a tree but with thick clumps of aloes and cactus. Surrounding it was the woodsy plain of the Hamma. In the background the green, shadowy Sahel was on one side and on the other the sea, with Algiers appearing along with it at sundown. In the east was the tag end of the mountains of Kabylia; above there was a cloudless sky and the sun, god for idolaters and the real king of the feast.

The men were packed together in a massive group like a huge flock on the sandy banks of the stream. The dances began near noon and lasted until nighttime. Given all the volunteers to replace musicians and exhausted dancers, the infernal music didn't stop for a minute. During that time the women set themselves up under the tents or nearby, and then everybody ate.

Considered the one official personage, the *amin* of the blacks in Algiers had at the center of the encampment a pavilion topped with standards that was more luxurious than any other. He's a small, slight man with a curly beard and a penetrating gaze. He had all the customary diplomacy and was serious yet affable. He offered coffee to those seeming to merit that honor. Being around so much where he was, I undoubtedly seemed to be someone notable since he invited me.

I bravely waited until evening. I saw the sun going down behind the hills. In the midst of the crowd and with all the music I set out for home, worn down by fatigue, sated with colors but extremely happy with my day. I imagined that I had laid away a stock of light for the overcast, all too frequent days when the mind sees only sad things.

Mustapha d'Alger

NAMAN IS dead. Naman the smoker of hashish, the man I spoke to you about last November, whose end I foresaw as his life was being burned up in the bowl of a pipe. Yesterday in the military training field I saw him pass by on a stretcher covered with red cloth. He was carried by his friends and neighbors, who following custom relieved each other every other minute, going at a fast clip. By neighbors I mean those from the café for Naman had no other home than the smoky café at Sid-Mohammed-el-Chériff. Having recognized the usual figures from that spot at the crossroads I paid attention to the burial procession and thus knew that it was that poor devil, who'd already been half dead for a long time and was now completely dead. He had kept to his ways, dreaming, sleeping, and smoking in the same place, breathing in no other life-giving air than that smoke. He was neither gayer, sadder, nor more self-contained than usual. They'd seen him that morning take his pipe and light it; and so he continued until noon. That evening they noticed that he was no longer smoking. His pipe had gone out—his life as well.

I wanted to join the very small number of those who made up the cortege and so followed them to the cemetery. The ceremony was short. He passed through the marabout where they generally undress the dead and which serves as a vestibule to the tomb site. I saw him reappear almost right away, carried in their arms, wrapped only in a winding sheet. Two grave diggers were making the hole, more or less as in *Hamlet:* one in the trench digging it; the other lifting the dirt out with a basket. Once the hole was dug they let the cadaver slip down into it; then it was the earth's turn. Ten minutes later the grave had been filled, creating a mound as if there'd been a furrow. You no longer knew what had been put there, whether it was a man or some seed.

If Naman didn't leave an heir, which is likely, and if his pipe is in the *kaouadji*'s hands, I'll buy it, and one day you'll see that murderous object.

P.S. Nothing new here. I went down to the crossroads where I saw Sid-Abdallah, who thought I'd left for France. He didn't mention Hawa. It moved me to see my house again, my prison of the past winter and the garden where the trees are in bloom. The prairie is no longer a lawn but a field ready to be reaped. The grass

Mustapha d'Alger

comes up to the bellies of the cows. The countryside is impregnated with the odor of haying. I don't have any reason to stay in Mustapha. Vandell is waiting for me at Blidah and I leave tomorrow.

Blidah, May

SEVERAL DAYS have passed now since I wrote you from Algiers. I spent them working as hard as I could, shut up in that small town where the air is humid. The warm weather there would wear down the strongest man with its irresistible urgings to take it easy. That's what remains of its seductive ways left over from the old days, a kind of physical well-being and forgetfulness of self that actually resembles a protracted bath. It's now the fifteenth of May, in other words summer. The days are long and it's heavy at midday. To live in harmony with the climate you have to take advantage of the mornings and the evenings, which are temperate, and dedicate the middle of the day to sleep.

Vandell left here yesterday. He told me he was not going far and won't be away long. Since he didn't warn me that he was going, I was most surprised as I woke up before dawn and saw him at the door of my room. He was finishing packing as he rolled up his traveling gear in his burnoose.

"So where are you going?" I yelled to him.

"I'm off," he said. "I thought about it last night and decided that I'm growing slothful and am taking on bad habits. I really can't tell you where I'm going, but I'm going. Even if I don't write, don't expect me before the middle of July. If you yourself take a trip, leave the key with Bou-Diaf."

Bou-Diaf is the most respected Arab hotel keeper on the rue des Koulouglis and is the usual landlord of Vandell when he comes to Blidah. His name is worthy of a proper sign for it means "father of the guest."

A half hour later Vandell returned with his white mare. He strapped his modest baggage on the beast's back, climbed in the saddle, and left. I found the house empty and, being now all alone after having been two, understood that I too had also been acquiring what Vandell stoically calls "bad habits."

same date, nighttime

THIS EVENING I explored the city—I'm beginning to say "I" again. I followed the contour of the ramparts from the outside starting out in the plain and going up to where the mountain begins. It was six o'clock when I went out and about nine where I came back to the point of departure, which shows you that I was walking slowly and stopped often. The evening was warm and the air very still. A welcome fog descended over the plain early on; the lake and marshes soon were outlined by streaks of white vapor. Swallows, which are too numerous to count in Blidah, bit by bit disappeared from the sky and the day lost its color. The air was full of flying nocturnal insects and mosquitoes.

When I reached the western gate I found a whole encampment around the watering troughs—fifty camels and around thirty camel drivers. Already it was no longer light, but by their manner, dress, darker complexion, more piercing eyes I could tell that they were from the Sahara.

"Where are you coming from?" I asked, and one of them answered, "From El-Aghouat."

El-Aghouat . . . as said by an Arab it's a word that's hard and full of character because of the guttural "gh," the equivalent of the Spanish "j." I listened to this strange name and had him repeat it to have the pleasure of hearing it again. It was the first time an Arab pronounced it in my presence with the proud and tender accent that's natural for someone talking to a stranger about the place he's from.

He told me, "Ten days to Boghar and from Boghar two days to Médéah."

"And what's the trail like?"

Mustapha d'Alger

He then gestured in the extravagant Arab fashion designating for my benefit the unbroken road that passed near the encampment, stretching out his arm in an indefinite way to express the interminate distance of an immense journey.

"Look, out there's the Sahara," as if nothing in the world was so beautiful for a man to look upon than the undefined emptiness of a flat horizon.

"Good evening and peace to all!"

"Peace to you!" replied the man from El-Aghouat.

And I resumed my walk.

Before going home, I went and sat down in the café at Bou-Djima. It's a small country café situated outside the city almost in the middle of the orange trees and surrounded on all sides by streams, as if a tiny island. There was no one. Bou-Djima was sleeping next to the ovens beneath the flickering lantern. I didn't wake him up and sat down before the entrance door. Here and there in the distance you could see points of light appearing and disappearing on the mountain and hear the barking of dogs from random spots. Then I looked at the sky where all the summer constellations were shining. The memory of the men from the Sahara instead of growing weaker would not leave me and without willing it, I started on a trip. Now when I travel, whether dreaming or in reality, it's always in the same direction, due south.

It's midnight. Nothing's worked out but it's possible I'll wake up tomorrow, as Vandell did yesterday, and quickly decide to hit the road.

4

The Plain

I'M JUST BACK from the south, having completed what I call—perhaps stretching things—a curious journey. That journey is set down almost day by day and step by step in a journal[18] that is independent of this one. The journal stops at El-Aghouat with the cry of a man who's parched after nearly three months of continuous thirst. I returned having been vanquished, as I admit, by that killing thirst. I was driven back north by an unknown, unreasoning desire to see cool water, to drink it, to plunge into it.

It took me fewer than six days on the road to do what it took us ten to do in going. I traveled nonstop without sleeping, walking day and night, no longer stopping for any length of time and never camping for more than a couple of hours. I'd found that the springs had dried up; there was mud rather than water or, what is even worse, a residue of greenish foam. I was wearing my horse out, and though I was exhausted, I was sustained to the very end by the certitude that I would spring back to life once we'd arrived. I stopped keeping track of the temperature after leaving El-Aghouat. I do remember that the thermometer registered 49.9 degrees centigrade at four o'clock the day of my departure. The priest there had himself handed me the current reading just as I was climbing into the saddle. It's a document that I'm keeping as corroboration of weather that in the last few days has seemed unbearable.

Having left El-Aghouat on a Sunday—after vespers as we'd say in a Christian land—I got to Boghari by Friday morning at eight-thirty. I went straight to the caravansary and settled in. I spent the day with my servant and camel drivers, stretched out on a hard platform under the courtyard's overhang where it wasn't much cooler than in the sun. That evening a rider entered the courtyard of the *foundouk;* it was Vandell. He'd learned of my departure, then of my setting out to return, coming to meet me at Boghari well aware that I wouldn't show up at Boghar.

"Congratulations," he said looking me over, "for once you look like a traveler!"

"My dear friend," I answered, "I'm dying of thirst." I then looked at him as if the mere sight of a friend coming from the north could quench my thirst.

The next day at three-thirty in the morning the moon was still shining, and with just a suggestion of daylight, together we set forth again on the road to Médéah. Both of us had used those three months of absence well, he in increasing his erudition and I in studying.

"Who made you decide to leave?" he asked.

I didn't tell him that I was following his example. I merely talked to him about the fortuitous encounter with the Saharans from El-Aghouat.

"And what did you see there?"

"Summer," I told him.

"That's a little vague," objected Vandell, "but we all have our own point of view."

The haying was long over; in the Oued-el-Akoum valley I could now only see an unchanging stretch of dry and once again powdery earth. The sun had devoured whatever stubble was still left. The heat was extreme even under the cover of the trees at the foot of the mountain and the pine trees gave off a suffocating odor of resin. The calls of the grasshoppers combining with the rasping of the sun-scorched branches surrounded us with a crackling, firelike noise. We had to push on until two o'clock to find a spring worthy of that name.

It formed a pool of deep, clear, cool water shaded by some very big trees. The spring lay as if in a basket in the middle of oleanders in full bloom.

"You see," I tell my Saharan *bach'amar* (caravan leader) that's what the water is like in my country."

The *bach'amar* drank a mouthful from the hollow of his hand, tasting it as he would some beverage unknown to him. Looking at the rocky, spiraling trail that climbed the dark flanks of the slope and the trees that were not palms, said, "God does well what he does."

I thought the same as he, my friend, and when the first enthusiasm of drinking subsided, said to the Saharan, "You're right, your country is the most beautiful in the world."

The eleventh day after my departure from El-Aghouat I arrived home at the moment that the cypress that I used as a sundial marked a little after four P.M.

Blidah, August

"WHERE ARE you coming from?" Hawa asked when she saw me.

"The south," I said, mentioning El-Aghouat.

"My father's from the Sahara," she threw in with the kind of matter-of-factness of some philosopher—a Spinoza—with whom one discusses Paradise. "And why did you leave me?"

I returned to my accustomed place on her divan and answered, "To let you have your summer siesta."

I found her as she was three months ago, only even a touch more languorous and noticeably less covered. Aichouna, whom I'd inquired about, spends a part of her evenings at *bitab*, which are little parties held at night, half an occasion for seeing dancing, half for listening to music. They say she's a great success as a dancer. Hassan the barber shared with me how much my sudden departure and my long absence had worried him and to bolster the effect of his words he mixed into his defective vocabulary French locutions such as "my dear friend" and "'dum' it!" As for Ben-Hamida, the scribe, I ran into him the day after my arrival. He was charming, fresh, rested—like a girl who's just come from her bath. Wearing a long gown of a delicate hue, he paraded elegantly, a fan in his hand.

"Good looks, good luck," Vandell said to him, to compliment him on how he looked.

Ben-Hamida questioned me about my trip, the probable future of a French settlement at El-Aghouat, and the mood of the people in the Sahara and the position they were taking. He wanted to know what was being said about a certain sheriff who was a southern agitator and why he was a cause of concern. All this was done with the curiosity natural to an enlightened man who's interested in the politics of his country. When I assured him that El-Aghouat under our control was going to be a substantial and perfectly secure frontier post; that the land there was healthy, habitable, and that after having been taken in spite of the Arabs, we would be able to keep it even with its climate, he was content to smile, replying with exquisite impertinence, "Extremely important men have choked on a fly."

And straight off he took leave of us.

Observing him depart so unceremoniously, I commented, "That devil of a man fights like a Parthian."

"Yes," Vandell said, "tossing proverbs. Pity he turned heel so quickly. I would have given him back ten."

Now that I've seen summer in its own home—in its kingdom —it has nothing more to teach me. I'm expecting no new thrill from a relatively changeable climate where the sun, like a bird of passage, has a season for appearing and one for migrating. The weather is beautiful but it's not the same kind of beauty as in the south; it's very warm but it's a warmth that's even gentler than before. While it's very dry, this dryness isn't comparable to that threatening aridity, which is as old as the world and guards the approaches of the Sahara. Here you can still see running streams, a lake that sends up vapors at night, and marshes where water is evaporating. The horizon is full of things in every direction and the sky is of a blue resembling velvet, not bronze. Furthermore, harvest time is over; grass and crops have been stored away, the plain is naked, September approaches. Autumn can come starting today.

A bit sadly, I put my journal in order along with my travel sketches for everything that is not very beautiful appears mediocre compared to what's down there and everything that's no longer empty, small. Blidah is a kind of Normandy—humid—and is good to visit when you're coming from Europe. It's wrong to stay here when returning from the south; its like going from the great to the pretty. There's no orchard, not even an African one, to rival an oasis and the desert puts the vastest plains to shame.

Day breaks between four and five o'clock. Involuntarily, I wake up as soon as it's light, another habit brought back from the land where sleep doesn't have a timetable and where you never fall completely asleep. My room fills in a confused way with light that bleaches things, and vague noises. I see dawn spreading above the green line of the wooded horizon. I listen: there's reveille, a tune that during two months set my heart to beating, a tune like no other when it's associated in your memory with poignant, unique sensations. Horses are neighing, camels belling; I hear barefooted people passing softly beneath my window; a roving breeze that precedes the sun has the orange trees nearby gently rustling; the air is lukewarm, the morning calm. Am I still in the Sahara? It's an illusion I have every morning, lasting just a moment, just long enough for me to recognize where I am and to realize I no longer have a mosquito net over me like a winding sheet, that I breathe freely, and that the buzzing of flies has halted: after which I find myself back here in another world. I wake up feeling at ease; and yet I detect some secret anguish, a feeling of possible danger buried in this sensation of peace. Life is agreeable, the climate healthy, and the season clement. It's then that I experience a bizarre regret and I watch with indifference the days unfold, no longer possessing anything to challenge me.

That's the way my days begin—with noises, a glow of light, forms half seen, the grayish beams of the dawn through my open window, by a greeting offered from my soul's depths to the things awakening at the same time as myself. It's not my fault if nature invades everything I write to such a degree. I accord it here at the very most the part that it plays in my life. This means to act in concert with live impressions, to produce without ceasing; to be in correspondence with what surrounds us; to serve as a mirror for things outside us, but voluntarily and without being their creature; finally, to make of our destiny what poets make of their poems, that is, to encase vigorous action in reverie, to modify Terence's *"homo sum"* by saying "Nothing that's divine is strange to me." There, my friend, is what would be neither too much nor too little —that's what living should be.

I read just today a book published in Algiers around 1830, finding in it an unexpected detail that, insignificant as it is, nevertheless struck me. That book is *Sketches of Algiers* by the American consul general William Shaler.[19] It's the most precise, accurate, and best informed thing that's been written on the situation with the Algerian government during the curious period when that government of buccaneers interjected itself, or rather was injected in the disputes of the European powers, and converted from piracy to diplomacy. The author, having sojourned in the Regency since 1815, having witnessed the reign of Omar, and having been the recipient of confidences from Hussein Dey, completed his book in 1825 at the very moment when the war with England was about to start up again. The situation had become serious, an English squadron blocking the city and threatening to bombard it anew.

From his consular post Shaler observed the preparations for war, keeping up with what was going on in the roads, making precise notes on any movements in the port. He noted the arrival of ships, their number, armament, and disposition. He also indicated atmospheric conditions, the winds and temperature, and then combined intelligence from the Kasbah with all that. From the piles of notes made day by day, hour by hour, he put together a thoroughly original journal, a kind of panoramic history that comes alive through its precision. In addition, the point of view makes it picturesque as well.

Dated June 14, 1825, here's what that observer wrote: "This evening, as a contrast to the din of war, and the anxiety naturally produced by impending hostilities in such a country as this is, we were gratified with the spectacle of one of the most interesting phenomena in the economy of nature. A *Cactus grandiflorus*[*sic*] in this garden began to bloom at sunset, and gradually expanding its ephemeral glory in a bright moonlight, filled the air, for many yards around, with its fragrant breath, in which the vanilla was sensibly predominant.

"15th. During the greater part of this day, the horizon was covered with a dense fog, the thermometer not rising above seventy-eight degrees, and the wind northerly. At about five in the evening, the haze partially clearing away, sixteen sail of British vessels were discovered in the offing. The beautiful flower that bloomed last night, was found closed this morning; it withered and died before evening."

And the following day the diplomat continues his account of the blockade. A minor detail noticed by chance illustrates in my opinion the composition of this book. The fog when the weather is hot, that rare plant that flowers during the summer night, remaining open only a few hours, contain a whole landscape. Superfluous details? I think not. They localize things, forcing you to remember the physical Algiers that gets forgotten, grounding history without its losing anything of its serious purpose. Were I ever to be the historian of a political or military event, you can be well assured that unconsciously I'd find a way during the course of the dry dust of politics, or in the middle of the incidents on a battlefield, to have something bloom like the cactus grandiflora of Shaler, the American consul.

September

WE'VE TAKEN up again the life you know all about, in the same environment and the same house, not varying from the patterns established by long habit. We are at work. Vandell has gone back to geology. He doesn't leave the house any more without his pick hammer, and wherever we go together he starts smashing rocks by the wayside like a road mender. I help him carry his samples with which he has blanketed the floor of his room. He spreads them out there to classify them, apparently without foreseeing that sooner or later we'll have to move. He brought back from his last outing a group of extremely curious drawings: profiles of mountains, rock formations with all the details of their interior stratification. Nothing could be more precise, cleaner or more minutely done. Every contour is indicated in a childlike way using such a free stroke as if done with the sharpest of burins. Shadows and highlights, naturally, don't exist; you've got the architecture of things rendered independently of the air, coloring, effects, in a word everything that represents life. It's coldly expository like a drawing in geometry. Not attaching the same *artistic* importance to his drawings (that he himself calls "Plans") he's surprised when occasionally I have trouble recognizing the site, wanting to argue with me over exactitude. I willingly accept the exactitude but deny the resemblance, or rather, the purported resemblance, denying its truthfulness. That's the starting point for a dissertation that led us into theories tending, you can well imagine, to the most opposite conclusions.

"All the same," he said to me today, "you have to explain to me what it is you're really hoping to make of this country. Sometimes

I hear you saying that it's curious, at others that it's beautiful; you speak first of naïvety and then of preconceptions; you invoke independence and traditions. You've always got one foot here and the other in some museum. Succinctly put, I watch you making a dangerous leap, and so must ask you directly whether you can possibly keep your balance."

"My dear friend, one of the weaknesses of our times is attempting what the strongest had never endeavored, not from timidity but out of wisdom, that is, putting great resolve into pipe dreams. There was a time when things were less complicated, with more men possessing greatness, perhaps because they were less complicated. In any case, the goal stood out and the means with which to reach it were few in number. We pretend that the goal is the same, but given the myriad paths observed with each of us making a fresh detour to get there, I doubt it. We didn't think that there was anything else except what we ourselves saw every day: beautiful human forms equaling beautiful ideas, or beautiful landscapes, that is, trees, water, fields, and sky. The air, the earth and water, three elements out of four, that was already a great deal. That was enough. We gave everything its approximate color and every form was expressed in the most appropriate way and not modified. We relied on a very modest but most worthy principle that divides works of art equitably into two parts, allowing nature the responsibility to be beautiful, reserving for us the right to conceive and reveal that beauty. Calling that operation of the mind the rendering of beauty or creation is only a partial mistake—but perhaps that's wrongly put."

After this rather formal introduction getting me into the presentation of principles that I'd neither looked for nor prepared, I continued, my friend, with my explanations. I wandered and using facts as corroboration, invoked the example of two painters whom we call "masters," all without much order or method, which won't surprise you.

"What we've lost," I said in more or less these terms, "is the proper interest in and taste for detail. We've been noting that for a long time yet the loss is irremediable. In the old days man was everything. A human face was worth a poem. When nature appeared behind a human being it was as a kind of backdrop taking the place of the dark background of portrait painters or the gold of the Italian primitives. Painting and sculpture went hand in hand to the point where painting appeared to be helped along by its elder sister. Still displaying fully the elements of their common origin and common development, painting continued to have the sense of individuality, the abstract, rounded relief of statuary. In the high Italian Renaissance the family ties of those twin arts were such that the man who brought them together, and nearly combined them in his works, has accordingly remained the greatest artist in the world. If less perfect than the Greeks, he was more inclusive. For me *The Last Judgment* is nothing but an immense bas-relief with movement and color. The day when a separation took place art was diminished. It was transformed the day that the *subject* was introduced into painting; and it declined for good the day that will be forever deplored when the *subject* and the *genre* destroyed great painting, denaturing even landscapes.

"The *subject* has been around for a long time and the *genre* as well. If we sincerely wished to go back to the beginnings, we'd perhaps be lacking in respect for some singularly venerable names. I'd be afraid to even mention them. We've always been too intellectual in France. That disposition was the misfortune of our great men. We might attribute more genius to the man who was 'king'[20] of the eighteenth century if he had been less intelligent, and yet we don't particularly notice that the greatest painter of the seventeenth century was himself as intellectual as he was intuitive.[21] Good sense, intelligence, acuity, and logic are just those Gallic traits that the Italians don't possess—or have never revealed. That's why Poussin is modern. He's that way in spite of his training and his exquisite feel for classical art. For all his having lived and died in Rome he remained at bottom a Norman from the Andelys, a neighbor of Corneille and a relative of La Fontaine. No matter how hard he tried, with all his *gravitas* he's an intellectual. He's very intent yet he uses his brain. His eye is good, as is his sense of the pathetic and the didactic. And he is after all a bit naive in the ordinary sense which the ancients gave to that term, that is, an uncomplicated, strong, ingenuous plastic sense. Very great art does not reason, at least not in the direction of syllogisms. It conceives, dreams, sees, feels, expresses: a simple and more naive procedure. What is the *subject* if not the anecdote introduced into art, the fact rather than the painterly idea, the story when there's a story, the scene, the exactness of dress, lifelike effects, in a word, truth whether historical or picturesque? Everything can be explained and everything proceeds by plan. The logic that is a component of the *subject* leads straight to local color, in other words, to an impasse for once you've reached that point, art might as well come to a halt, its finished.

"Religious history, the Ancient and New Testaments with their elevated thoughts dealing with faith based in belief, by their remoteness in legend, by the mysteries involved in the deeds described were lifted above the anecdotal and became part of what is epic. But on what condition? On the condition of being the *credo* of an enraptured soul as was the case of the monk of Fiesole[22] or being poured into the mold of a sublime form as was the case of Leonardo, Raphael, Andrea del Sarto—those pagans. The *subject* wasn't for them anything more than the opportunity to represent the apotheosis of man in all his attributes. As soon as the arrangement of the thing being painted becomes too explanatory one of two things happens: in the first case, the *subject* becomes transfigured as in the hands of the Venetian colorists cum draftsmen. By the absence of any *true* color, by the disregard for history and chronology, it serves as a pretext for an epic fantasy where deep down it passes unnoticed. Or, in the second case, the intention to remain faithful gets the upper hand and art is quickly dwarfed. The way in which the Venetian scenographers understood the *subject* makes it easy to see the mediocre case they made for it. When Titian paints *The Burial of Christ* what does he see? A contrast— the plastic idea—a white body, dead, livid, being borne by men in red and mourned—bereavement rendering them more beautiful —by tall Lombard women with reddish hair: that's how the *subject* was understood. You observe that the interest in being *true* wasn't great and the wish to be new didn't go any further that being exact. To be beautiful was the first and last consideration, the alpha and omega of a catechism we scarcely know today.

"Suddenly about twenty years ago after having exhausted ancient history, and then local history, from fatigue or whatever, painters started off anew. From that period we can date a quite unexpected movement. I'm talking here about the need for adventure and the taste for travel. Now please note that we travel at the point when we've become interested in nature's diversity. Distance isn't a factor. You can go no farther than Saint-Denis yet nevertheless bring back from the banks of the Seine works that I'd describe as travel notes. You can, on the other hand, go around the world and only produce more general works, impossible to situate, bearing neither stamps nor kilometer markings. They're quite simply paintings. In a word, two kinds of men exist whom you mustn't confuse: there's the traveler who paints and there's the painter who travels. And the day when I know positively that I'm either one or the other, I'll tell you exactly what I intend to do with this country."

We'd arrived by this point in Market Square. A gang of native children were engaged in a game that requires skill and agility. Our own schoolboys are practiced at it for I believe it to be international, being found in Ireland as well as in the Orient. The game consists in knocking around a ball or a stick, or something that is light and can be easily be sent a distance. Each player is equipped with a stick and whoever gets there first hits the object. The players were young children between eight and twelve. They had pleasant faces, and like most Moorish boys supple limbs, fine features, big, beautiful eyes, and a complexion that would be the envy of a woman. Their arms were bare, their delicate necks poking out of vests that were worn open; the legs of their wide pantaloons were rolled up to the knee to help them run better; and a little red *chachia* like the skullcap of a choirboy just barely crowned the top of their pretty bald heads. Each time the ball was intercepted and thrown again, altogether they would throw themselves in pursuit, jostling side by side like so many gazelles. They gesticulated a great deal as they ran, paying no attention as they lost hats and belts. As they tore toward the goal, you never saw their feet touching the ground. The fleetness of their feet as they ran made you aware only of naked heels whipping about in the billowing dust, that aerial cloud appearing to add to their speed and carry them forward.

It was two o'clock. The market had just ended and the square was deserted. A block of low, flat-roofed houses; one or two cypresses pointing on high above the terraces; beyond that the mountain whose saw-toothed profile on the horizon shared more than half the sky; then a large, flat stretch of country: so much for the landscape. The houses were flat white, the paint in quite good condition; the cypresses black. The mountain was of a decided green; the sky a bright blue; and the ground was the color of dust, that is, a sort of lilac. In the midst of the bright light there was a solitary shadow outlined on the side of the square where the sun was already going down, and that shadow bathed in the sky's reflection could also have been designated by a blue.

"You can make out all right," I said to my companion, "this square and the children, can't you? The scene is familiar, presenting the conditions required for genre. The setting has as well the double virtue of going well with it, all the while being quite local. Let's take the example of this picture that seems done in advance and as easy to copy as to describe. One example is as good as another. If necessary, the Orient can be restricted to an equivalent narrow conception.

"Yet to begin with—if you'll let me be pedantic in my way—

what do we see? Are those children playing in the sun? Is it a sunny square in which children are playing? The question is not pointless for it establishes primarily two very different points of view. In the first case it's a painting of figures where the landscape is considered an accessory; in the second it's a landscape where the human figure is subordinated, placed in the background where its role is sacrificed completely. Any number of opinions can immediately occur from those questions. Everyone will answer them according to his own temperament and understanding, as well as by the way he looks at things and the direction in which his talent lies. The landscape painter will see a landscape, the figure painter a subject. One will distinguish spots of color, another how figures are dressed, while yet a third will study the overall effect, and a fourth will see gestures in it. For yet another it may be facial expression. Depending on whether we envisage them from near or far the children will become everything or nothing at all. If we suppose that they are very near the painter so that the portrait of each of them takes on a dominant interest, then a considerable modification will appear in this quite simple picture. The entire landscape will disappear altogether; at most we'll vaguely be aware of something like a sunlit plot of ground and some indications of an Oriental setting. The only thing left that is visible and coherent will be a group of children caught up in rapid movement and joyous emotion. They are presented in such a way as to display the expression of the gestures with some, with others the interplay of physiognomies. Eliminating as we go, we get to the point where the background is reduced, then eliminated, thus enlarging the group and then simplifying it. Dress becomes incidental and secondary in a subject whose interest is concentrated to such a degree on human forms and faces, and right away we eliminate the sun and the excessive light, a double obstacle that nobody in the world would have been bothered by when the test was to paint a group of people.

"What then happens to the very site where the scene is we're now taking in? That white square, those black cypresses, the white sun of the noon hour—what becomes of all the local surroundings which have their meaning and which are essential if we wish to localize the scene? Unless, on the contrary, we wish to generalize it.

"Here we touch upon abstractions. Without wishing it, by the mere fact of a more demanding, focused point of view, we leave nature behind and deal with calculations straight out of the painter's studio. We abandon relative truth for a larger category of truth that's less precise yet really closer to the absolute for being less particular. For me that square in Blidah, off by itself in the extreme brilliance of the full light of a beautiful summer's day, those red vests and white trousers, the pretty children who are out of the ordinary—and that's the characteristic that bewitches us—the heat, the noise, the diversity of the scene in its changes from moment to moment, all that makes up an ensemble of multiple impressions. It charms us for that reason, especially since we observe within it a painting of the Orient's particular character. On the other hand, there are painters, and I know some, who would only take from the scene what is strictly necessary. They would judge to be of greatest interest not that these are little boys from Blidah but that they are children. And you couldn't accuse them of not being right.

"This intellectual method consists in selecting a point of view, deciding on the scene, and isolating it in the midst of what it's a part of. The purpose is to sacrifice background detail by making you imagine it rather than showing it; to take care to explain what has to be explained and leaving to be assumed what's accessory. This is the art of indicating things elliptically and getting the viewer to imagine what he doesn't see. It's the great art of making use of nature without stereotyping it, at times copying it in a most literal manner, at other times almost seeming to forget about it. There's exists a difficult balance in what appears real that requires you to be true without being precise, to paint and not describe, to give not illusions but impressions of life. This process translates into an ordinary word, which is the cause of much misunderstanding because it's never been well defined: 'interpretation.'

"The question boils down to knowing whether the Orient lends itself to being rendered, the degree to which this is admissible, and whether to interpret it isn't to destroy it. I'm not creating a paradox, just taking a close look and I'm not creating an objection, just pointing it out. Believe me, it hurts me to talk so offhandedly about a land to which I owe much.

"The Orient is very special. It's great drawback for us is that it's unknown and new. To begin with, it arouses a feeling alien to art, curiosity, which is most dangerous and that I'd like to ban. The Orient is exceptional, but history attests to nothing beautiful or durable having been created with exceptions. It disregards the basic laws, the only ones worth following. Finally, it talks directly to the eyes, less to the intellect. Nor do I think it capable of moving us, meaning those of us—and that's the greatest number—who haven't lived there. In order to understand it they haven't a close familiarity with its customs or perhaps fond memories of it. Even when it's very beautiful, it retains something that resists us, that's exaggerated, violent, and seemingly excessive. This is an order of beauty without precedents in either ancient literature or art and which strikes you as bizarre at first.

"In addition, it impinges with its characteristic many-sidedness and singularity. There's the way of dressing; the oddity of its different physical types; the harsh impression it can offer; the particular rhythm of its lines; the uncommon range of colors. If anything at all in that profile, so novel and uncompromising, were to be changed, it would be diminished. To tone down what is too vivid would be to make it dull; to generalize its image would be to disfigure it. We therefore have to accept it in its entirety. I challenge anyone to escape from the necessity of being true, that is, to begin by expressing the unusual aspects. Thus one is led by the very logic of sincerity to forced excesses of naturalism and facsimile reproduction.

"With either approach a similar aberration will definitely result.

"The painter who courageously selects the course of championing at whatever cost truthfulness will bring back from his travels something so very unusual and difficult to categorize. Dictionaries of art don't have an appropriate term for works of such uncommon nature. I'd call that kind of production 'documents.' By that I mean the calling up of a land, what distinguishes it and makes it itself. It also makes it come alive for those who know it and makes it known to those who don't know it. For instance, there's the exact physical type of its inhabitants—some modified by African blood, for instance—or what is only of interest because of a certain extravagance—their customs, their way of walking, which isn't ours. A traveler's investigations have no limits once he's made it a rule to be exact. From the images and all their minutiae copied with the scrupulous authenticity of a portrait, we will see and know for sure just how a given people overseas dresses, what it puts on its head and on its feet. We'll learn what its weapons are, the painter rendering them as well as a paint brush can. We will have to know as well what the harnesses, etc. of his horses are like. What's more we will have to understand these things for along with the ingenious fabrication that goes into showing so many new things for the traveling painter there is linked the obligation to break things down, and in so doing explain them. The attraction of the unwonted corresponds to an unfortunate universal instinct of curiosity. Many people mistakenly will then require of painting that it provide exclusively a travelogue. They will want paintings that are composed like inventories, and the interest in ethnography will end up by becoming confused with the beautiful.

"With landscapes there'll be the same manifestations, less evident perhaps but no less real. The interest in faraway places is immense. There's an irresistible pleasure in saying about a country

The Plain

145

that few people have visited: I saw it. You know about that, you who've spent your life in discovering. First of all we have to be very modest—already that's a human virtue that's extremely rare—in masking our accomplishments as a traveler and not put place names next to the painter's name. We have to be even more modest—and that modesty becomes a principle of art—to be selective when painting in making use of all those precious notes, to sacrifice our own satisfaction with our own memories to the vague research for a general and uncertain goal. Let's not mince words, there has to be a veritable abnegation of self to conceal all our studying, revealing only the results.

"Yet the difficulty lies not only there: it's elsewhere, it's everywhere. What's difficult, and I repeat this, is to interest our European public in places that it knows nothing about. What's difficult is to show places so as to make them known, yet in the usual way we accept objects already familiar to us, thus to separate out the beautiful from the bizarre and the impression of a stage set that is almost always devastating—to manage to include the most risky novelties using common means of expression. The object is finally to obtain the result whereby this country, which is so particular, becomes a painting that's sensitive, intelligible, and believable. It will have accommodated itself to the rules of artistic judgment, exceptions becoming the rule without going beyond or falling short. Now, as we've said, the Orient is extraordinary—and I take this word literally. It eludes the conventions, it's outside any discipline; it transposes, it turns everything on its head; it upsets the harmonies that landscape has lived with for centuries. I'm not speaking here of a fictitious Orient that preceded the recent studies that have been made on the spot; I'm talking about a country of chalky dust that as it takes on color becomes a little garish and yet is a little sad when no strong colors enliven it. It appears uniform yet hides under that apparent unity of hues an infinite number of nuances and tonalities broken down; it has rigid forms that are more often placed horizontally rather than vertically, very well-defined, with no haze, no attenuation, almost without any appreciable atmosphere and no depth of distance. Such is the Orient that you and I know, that has surrounded us and that we've seen. With its fleeting linearity this is the country par excellence of what's big, light in color, and immobile—burning stretches of terrain under a blue sky, in other words, lighter in color than the sky. At any given moment, this results in—take careful note—pictures which are upside down for there's no center, light coming from all sides, and no mobile shadows since the sky is cloudless. Last, as far as I know, no one before me has ever been concerned with struggling against an essential obstacle which is the sun. No one has imagined that one of the goals of painting is to express—with those paltry means of which you're aware—the excess of light from the sun that builds up through diffusion. I point out to you here the practical difficulties; there are a thousand others which are more profound and serious and that merit being pondered even more.

"Three men in the past twenty years sum up more or less what modern criticism has called "Oriental painting." Of those three you know at least one, and his name is mentioned too often in France for you not to have heard some echo of it even in the wilderness spots you frequent. Even if it were just between me and you some four hundred leagues away in Paris, I wouldn't allow myself to judge these three. I'll only say, to use the currently fashionable phrases, that out of the Orient one made landscape, the second landscape and genre, while the third did genre and great painting.[23] Each one of them saw the Orient, and saw it well, and if not with uniform understanding at least with a love that was alive, sincere, and lasting. The ensemble of their works has been a revelation.

"The landscape painter started by visiting the most famous places on earth and describing them, signing each with the name of a city, village, or mosque. He treated them more or less as portraits and so was forced to give the name of the original. His work is exquisite and a perfect illustration of a trip for which he could have himself written the text since he brought to writing as to painting the same precision of eye, the same vivacity of style and expression. Out of all that considerable oeuvre now, the memory of which is already today somewhat blurred, what will remain, being the most luminous, select, and memorable, are the little paintings that don't have names and are without a precise designation, for example a *twilight* on the banks of the Nile or else some poor *pilgrims* traveling at noon surrounded by the arid atmosphere of a land without water. Two notes occur frequently with him, an impression of noctural melancholy and the terror of loneliness in the burning heat. I won't say that's what's most perfect in his work, for the clear-cut intelligence of the man and the skilled hand of the practitioner are visible in all paintings signed by him. They probably are, however, what he's left us that's the most felicitous, both as benefits his fame and honors modern art.

"The genre painter proceeded more resolutely. In the Orient he saw effects: the clean, accentuated, sharp contrast between light and shadow. Since he couldn't capture the sun directly—it burns all hands that seek it out!—he went around the problem in a very intelligent manner. Finding it impossible to express much sun when there are few shadows, he thought that with a lot of shadow he would be able to produce a little bit of sun, and he succeeded. Everywhere he sought out that abstraction of an effect, the unvarying theme of vigorous contrasts, in every subject whether a face or a landscape, obstinately, forcefully, and with a degree of success that legitimized his daring. He had considerable imagination, was a great dreamer, yet maintained a distance, operating within intellectual, methodological, and practical preconceptions. He's neither true (as we've defined it) nor realistic. If you'll allow me a barbarism straight out of the studio, he was *peu nature*. His superiority, which is uncontested, came as with all visionaries from having a mind that was fertile in transmutations. He invents more than he remembers. From his stays in the Orient he retained, I think, a kind of love of straight angles, squared-off horizons, abrupt intersections that make up the formula, the geometry so to speak of his art. Everything he's produced is recognizable in these two characteristics: the intensity of effect and the methodical combination of forms. Perhaps without his being aware of it, the subject is just a changing pretext for applying his formulas in an identical manner. Basically, if something is lacking in this very independent-minded art of his, it's that it goes too much in one direction and not enough in the other. In a word, he made enormous sacrifices to light as the indispensable justification of beauty.

"The third has climbed higher on the nearly endless ladder of great art. In the Orient he saw man as spectacle. Note well, I don't say just plain man. He saw the way mankind dresses and along with that the carriage, gestures, and the features (vaguely). He saw costumes and color wonderfully well. He in his turn made an abstraction of color. He so increased its role, he lent it such importance, drawing out such diverse, important, and striking meaning, even at times quite pathetic. He thus forced us to forget, so to speak, the form, making us suppose that he looked down on or was ignorant of it, two errors he is quite innocent of. Even for paintings done out of doors he imagined a sort of Elysian daylight which is steady, soft, moderate. I'd call it the chiaroscuro of the open countryside in virtue of the principle that color once broken down by harsh shadows as well as light loses the effect of fullness and its intense quality. He took the strong blues of the Orient's sky, its pale shadows, its soft halftones, at times letting fall on an open parasol something like the weightiness of a heavy, dreary ray of sun. More often he's at home with cold half light, the true light of Veronese, and substitutes without hesitation green fields for scorched horizons. This third painter takes the landscape as reference point, a kind of unheard, deep accompaniment that sets off, supports, and increases a hundredfold the magnificent sonority of his coloring. His masterpiece, at least in genre painting, is a painting of an interior. It's light in color—blond—limpid, and so cleanly transcribed that you'd say it had been executed with one stroke, in one breath.

The Plain

And this painting by its perfection gives precise testimony to how the man I'm speaking of understood the Orient: his love of costume, his scruples concerning just how things look, and finally, his scant interest in the sun and its effects. They say of his works that they're beautiful but imaginary; they'd prefer him to be truer, more naive, and perhaps they'd even like him to be more Oriental . . . but never listen to people who talk like that. You should instead believe that what is most beautiful with him is their most common feature.

"The landscape painter, through who knows what singular predestination, was born a painter of the Orient. They say he looked like an Arab. The genre painter has a liking for the Ottoman countries because of their exoticism. The painter of historical scenes is a 'Venetian' who takes pleasure in contemporary subjects having colors analogous to those of the masters he remembers with such fervor. He's therefore the most traditional and the least Oriental of the three; but that's the least of my reasons for judging him to be so great.

"One spring day I was on the banks of the Seine with a famous landscape painter who had been my teacher.[24] He was explaining to me the changes that experience, study in museums, and above all trips to Italy had brought about in his way of seeing and feeling things. He told me that currently he perceived only the essence of things where before he was enchanted by details. After having sought out the particular, he now looked for the typical in both form and idea. A shepherd passed by leading a flock of sheep that trailed along the river's edge. The loose-gaited sheep were seen in profile against the water turned whitish by the gray sky of late April. The shepherd, his pouch over his shoulder, had a black felt hat and a herder's leather gaiters; by his side trotted two picturesque black dogs. The flock proceeded in an orderly fashion. 'You know,' my teacher said, 'it's a lovely thing to paint a shepherd on the banks of a river.' The Seine had changed names just as the subject had changed through the way it was approached: the Seine had become 'a river.' Who among us can make of the Orient something individual while at the same general enough to become the equivalent of that simple idea of a river?"

That's more or less what I said to Vandell. Draw what conclusions you wish from this chaos of views, caveats, and jumbled notes. I've been reporting on a discussion, not a rule book or even a chapter from a work of criticism.[25] The personal conclusion that I drew from it was that it's probable that I'll fail in what I undertake but that won't prove that the task can't be accomplished.[26] It's also possible that I'm influenced by a contradiction common to many and am attracted by the very peculiarities that I condemn, what's accessory becoming more important than ideas and instinct being preponderant over theory.

October

WE'VE AGREED to leave tomorrow on a hunting expedition to last three or four days. We'll be beating the countryside around Lake Haloula as well as the hills that lead to Tipaza, where we'll shoot rabbit along the old Roman road.

Commandant —— will be leading the hunt; our companions will be old Africa hands, officers in the native cavalry who are known to be excellent shots. And to let you know immediately the military allure of our expedition, we are taking along as servants, honor guards, or escorts, according to circumstances, ten red-caped spahis who are stationed at Blidah. The convoy (which could be a bit more modest) will be made up of two wagons pulled by four horses each. The dogs, whom they want to spare for the following day, will ride in the wagons along with the camping gear, baggage, and the arsenal of hunting rifles and ammunition, which it's planned will allow a minimum of a hundred shots per hunter. Finally, a further detail allowing you to judge the massacre that's being organized: we are taking along three big bread sacks meant to contain the game not consumed on the spot plus any inedible waterfowl.

"Don't expect," Vandell said informing me of customs surely little known outside of Algeria, "to proceed cautiously as you would in France making little noise. Here the dogs are only used to spot the trail. Once the prey has been found, the hunter takes care of the rest, firing off his rifle for as long as the bird's in the air, chasing it on horseback from spot to spot, tiring it, forcing it into the open, trampling it when it's completely worn out. This rather original combination of chase and shoot will surprise you, I believe. The combination makes for two exciting tests of skill: sharpness of eye and speed. Nothing out there will be spared, neither the terrain, which belongs to no one, nor the game, which is plentiful. Everyone is free to go all out as in enemy territory; the goal is to kill a lot. It's a practice acquired in war. That's why all the officers like hunting and are good at it, and by the same token every good rabbit and partridge man is by rights an excellent soldier for Africa. In both cases, the athletic skills are the same. We are assured that for a fairly hardy soul hunting is as good as war. Two pleasures, however, are lacking which nothing can replace: both sides being equal in the struggle plus danger's incomparable charm.

"I warn you about all that," Vandell added, "so that you'll know what you'll be up against tomorrow whether you wish to invest your pride in the endeavor or just want to go along on the chase as modest spectator. I'll be there riding my white mare." For Vandell his white mare is the only horse that lets him think his thoughts in peace.

I'll follow along tomorrow as I can, my friend, my sole desire being to see the lake, and you know why. The lake is one of the few things I'm really curious about (I'm embarrassed to be making much of such a trifle). We had planned this trip when you were here but never undertook it and since I'm offered the opportunity the least I can do is go and rectify or verify what together we had imagined it to be like. I'm going there as if on pilgrimage to salute an unknown thing from close up, going with the devotion owed an object left over from a old dream. All fantasy aside, while it's a small thing, it's good to replace a question mark—particularly one that's been standing there for years constantly pestering you with, "What's there—there?"—with a fact.

What's there, I'm sure, as everywhere is what we encounter at the end of the road after every rather long stage—the youthful enthusiasm of past years sprawled on the ground, so done in, alas, as to be comatose. Will the weather be nice tomorrow? That's what we're interested in. The south wind has been blowing a gale for five days now. This is the scorching good-bye of summer's dog days that come to an end in September. It's the stormy action of the equinox and also an alert to the fine weather of the season we are about to enter, which here they call "second summer." Elsewhere I've spoken about this dreadful wind. It's very beautiful to observe, and it stimulates the mind if your body isn't too enervated. The people of Blidah curse it; they suffer from it, protecting themselves as they can by staying at home, stuffing the windows and trying not to breathe. The heat has been extreme, not letting up day or night. Last night, and I have proof, it was 37 degrees centigrade under the orange trees at midnight, an extraordinarily high temperature for that hour in this season. I tried to imagine what the trees must suffer as I see them bent to the point of breaking in a struggle that's impossible to paint. They are embattled, almost torn apart by the wind that wants to rip them from the ground while roots hold them in a terrible bond they can't break. There was one point when everything seemed to crack; a kind of ripping noise came from down inside each tree. Let's see, I thought to myself, which will be the stronger, destruction or life. Life was stronger. Believe me, I was relieved: not one tree was uprooted, just thousands of twigs and leaves flying, gyrating through the air while half-ripe fruit in the hundreds rolled about in the road.

The Plain

Whether because of its flexibility or solidity, the cypress tree nearby bent like a reed and immediately righted itself without apparently having suffered in any way. When the wind started to blow steadily it stayed bent way over not straightening out until morning, the very hour when all of a sudden the gale died down. And yet, I who hate the wind, forgive this one, perhaps because of its source. I'll still say welcome to the desert wind as to everything that brings me news direct from the Sahara.

There's another particularity of this season that has a sort of threatening aspect. Every evening we see flames rising high over the plain. The Arabs are burning the brush, using this expeditious method to clear the land as quickly as possible without billhook or plow. The fire follows the direction of the wind, spreading from southwest to northeast. By day you see only wisps of smoke that you could mistake for fog. By evening flames appear again very clearly as the fire resumes its course; the horizon of the Sahel is lit up in a sinister way.

This evening the *khamsin* has completely died down as if by miracle. The sky is almost blue. The air is once again air and not that billowing dust. Goodnight then until tomorrow. The rendezvous point is Bab-el-Sebt at the appointed hour of six A.M. We can count on the sun, a wonderful companion who's never found lacking. You tell him, "See you tomorrow!" You can tell him, "See you next year!" And if anyone's to miss an appointment, he's not the one.

the encampment, Lake Haloula, October

WE'VE ARRIVED, and so I'm where I wanted to get to. The hunt begins tomorrow. Starting tonight, while our companions are readying themselves, I'll talk to you about crossing the plain, which was a mere short stroll. We took it very easy.

We left at exactly six o'clock accompanied by the rather noisy escort that I told you about. In all there were twenty-eight to thirty horses, making quite a racket, stirring up a tide of dust that was with us until we made it to brushland. The weather was wonderful, calm, and clear. There was a lot of humidity in the plain and, given that the sun is the greatest benefactor in the world after God, you would have thought that its light alone had changed the nighttime dew into silver rain. That glittering mirage fooling no one danced before our eyes for a brief hour; then the sun itself did what reality always does with lies, and the plain appeared as it is, not dead but arid, more unplowed than sterile, not wild but neglected by the hand of man. Actually, it resembles those cantons that you have to cross coming from Algiers; there's less brush than when you leave the Sahel, fewer marshes than around Bouffarik as well as more frequent moors. I mean by moors, here as elsewhere, everything that shoots up by chance everywhere the plow hasn't been; what the earth produces spontaneously when it hasn't been worked, fertilized, or planted with a crop, and that, even in this land where nature is generous, takes it easy as much as possible. Indestructible wild onions grow there intermixed with dwarf palm trees that will be the despair of future settlers; wild artichokes that are already visible with their colorless stems and bearded tops; rosemary, lavender, and yellow broom; finally, brush that's half lost the bit of thorny leafage that made it look as if it were stunted and that long ago took on the indefinable color of something powdery and inanimate. In that whole long stretch summer hasn't left any grass with life in it; in succession it's been beaten upon by the heavy rains, weighed down by stagnant water, hardened, broken up, and scorched by what have been already five months of drought and more or less continuous sun. Now the land is a vast empty space and to cross it is as soft to a horse's hooves as a freshly mown field. I'm ignorant as to what grew in those meadows without grass before the blazing sun or the teeth of whatever flocks obliterated them; but now you see only a multitude of huge, long-stemmed thistles, all of which like the staffs of Arab flags are crowned by a white pompom made up of silky fuzz. Nothing could be more sterile or strange. The summer breeze passes through that light-colored crop of numberless blooms without causing the least rustle; it disperses the bright-colored silk, broadcasting its useless seed over the miles of abandoned countryside. Land that's more barren is yet to come, where the marl is even more stripped of vegetation, and then at scattered intervals low-lying sections where the cool underground water makes the stiff, silent plant life of marshes issue forth with its sad greenery. All that is neither beautiful nor ugly. Insignificant details disappear in so vast an ensemble prodigiously bathed in light and air. The perspective, which is almost immeasurable, is nonetheless contained within a setting that's well-defined and clearly visible. The colors are so light and the shapes stand out so, it would be hard to imagine any more precisely greater indeterminate vastness. Indefinite space is reduced to the proportions of a picture, being soberly summed up within exact limits: a striking spectacle when you've only seen plains that are endless or too confined, in other words, the lack or the excess of size.

Elsewhere I've told you how when you cross that same plain a rise in the ground vanishes in the great emptiness. In the distance to the north you can make out rows of shrubbery that we'll be passing on our right and that in reality are woods. Then at long intervals there'll be a white mark of indeterminate shape, a little like a sheet forgotten in the countryside; it represents an isolated farm belonging to a French family; or even less often a series of somewhat rounded, blackish spots gathered together in some sort of order like piles of dead grass—a *douar*. When a tree appears on the flat horizon where your eyes have grown tired trying to break down the various blues, where greenery is lacking, where there's no shade at all it may be an old olive tree protected by local superstition. The childless women of the neighboring tribes come hang on it as ex-votos bits of cloth (now rags) torn from their veils. Or that tree may be an odd group of date palms growing out of the same clump as if wanting to keep each other company, tortured as they are by the effects of a harsh climate that's not their own. In the distance you can make out roads, all leading to Blidah; they're at such a distance that an army could be passing over them without your seeing it. Blidah rises up the farther the traveler goes away from it, down onto the lower levels of the plain. The city is then outlined more distinctly atop a small plateau clinging to the mountain; it offers a sharp, clear silhouette against the curtain of its gardens now tinged with blue.

By eight o'clock we passed over the Chiffa, which is dry, a thing that's hard to believe for those who've had to affront it during the rainy season. Nothing could be more inoffensive and pleasant: fine gravel, sand, a pretty Arcadian crown of oleanders that still had their star-shaped blooms, and two slender rivulets of water running out of sight in the wide, abandoned bed capable of holding a river. Two leagues from us on the left is the entrance to the gorge where these days a worn-out stream exits, and that has witnessed so many disasters.

At nine "powder spoke," but without great effect, being the sole rifle shots that, an insignificant preamble to the morrow's hunting. A flock of Carthage hens took off from the clumps of cactus cropping up in disorderly fashion around an abandoned tomb. They were quite far away by the time they'd heard the rumble of our wagons. The first volleys had been fired haphazardly. The winged band, feeling the wind off the shots, involuntarily swung away as if to let the lead pass them by. They then closed ranks, making a swift getaway. For a second the sun lit up the white plumage, then all was gone.

The Carthage hen or small bustard is a bird that's rare in France. Lots of hunters are keen for it. There's a reason for me to point this out in a correspondence that so seldom mentions hunting. It plays a part in festivities in our province at home along with a bird that's even more venerable, a hundred times rarer, almost legendary. I mean the big bustard. It's called the *houbara* here and the Arabs, who are the least interested in hunting of any group on earth, are fond of discussing it. Shaw[27] (who disputes its being the same thing as the bustard) describes the *houbara* thusly: pale yellow spotted with brown, whitish band around the neck with black stripes, flat beak like that of the starling, webbed feet. Bustard or not, it's a very handsome bird, even more beautiful by being impossible to find. It's especially desirable because when uncovered it's even more difficult to catch. One day in the Hodna, actually among the ruins of the Roman city of Tobna, I saw two of those uncatchable birds suddenly rising from among some stone shards but out of reach. As if chance had brought them together for a moment's friendship, the two solitary birds went each his own way. One went right, the other left, putting the desert between us and them. Nevertheless, a few days later a *houbara* was killed before my eyes. Here's how it happened. We were traveling in a column. There were trumpets in the vanguard, and so I don't know how the bird let itself be surprised and disoriented. Instead of fleeing before the column, it backtracked, all of a sudden appearing above the soldiers. It flew slowly and somewhat clumsily as if it had lost both any sense of caution or hope of escape, fright having gripped it. It crossed from the head to the very end of the small army; miraculously, it reached the rear guard without having been fired upon. There a kitchen hand who had seen it coming and took his time taking aim, dropped it two paces in front of his donkey. It was a magnificent bird the size of a small turkey, weighing four or five pounds. Its fluffed-up, whitish collar adorned its neck like a fluted ruff from the time of Henry IV.

At eleven we came to a halt in the bed of the Oued-Djer, a deep, clay-banked river dried up like the Chiffa of which it's a tributary. It had retained only one or two inches from its winter flow. We arrived to find a long line of cattle drinking below the steep banks lined with tamarisks, olive trees, and lentisks. Toward three we climbed back in the saddle to continue our trek over the plain. On our left we passed the Hadjout, whose tents we could see as well as their horses wandering about in herds just as in the Camargue. Some camels that had straggled away from the *douar* came close instead of fleeing and peacefully watched us go by. They were erect and rigid, all bones, with their hairy humps, backs loaded with firewood, callused knock-knees, big, soft feet, huge, strange rough-cut heads, mobile lips, and gentle eyes. Those big brown beasts at rest there between the colorless earth and a sky of tender blue doubled in proportions and volume, like an elephant seen up close, taking on something of the monumental interest of the extranatural: the whole plain (meaning ten leagues of vanishing perspective) was contained between their hocks. The silhouette of the high mountains outlined as if by a brush at the height of their stomachs comprised the background of this singular picture. They weren't grazing, there being nothing to graze on. They strolled about with an absent-minded, footloose, and (I'd say) bored air, that being the nature of these ruminants who aren't big eaters. The austereness of these animals takes on in an extraordinary way the significance of a moral quality: seeing that they are not the least bit hungry, we want to believe they're deep in thought.

That whole plain is a battlefield as the Hadjout are well aware. It's where skirmish after skirmish, little by little we won the interminable battle of Zama. Once plows arrive, once spades have turned over the soil where so much iron and so little wheat has been sown, we'll find reminders of our legionnaires, their swords, their shot as well as many skeletons.

Our only encounter today during the seven or eight hours on the road was with some shepherds, two youths plus an old man. The older of the two sons, a young man of around twenty, was watching a flock of fat-tailed sheep and black goats from atop a piece of tumbled-down wall, the last vestige of who knows what ruin, perhaps Roman, Vandal, Byzantine, Turkish, or Arab. An archaeologist could recount the history of these five great people by positing the possible origins of this bit of wall. The youth blew on a primitive reed pipe, drawing out of it not precisely music but rather sounds without harmony or rhythm. The wind carried the

The Plain

sound across the moors; a long-eared watchdog appeared to be moved by it for he began to yelp. Off to one side the old man went along, one arm supported by a big boy who was probably about sixteen. Both wore the narrow, short gown of shepherds: a jacket secured at the waist, hood in braided felt and sandals made of strips of leather cut from the skin of a lamb. The old man's eyes kept blinking, making me think he was blind. The young man was so handsome that as he passed near him, Vandell addressed him with a noble Arab greeting, "Greetings to you Jacob, son of Isaac, and greetings to your father!"

Could I have been wrong, my friend, when I once said that a living Bible is nowhere to be found?

A little later we were in a dense thicket of low-branching lentisks, broom, and tamarisks on the northwest side of the lake. Fire had gone through there and everywhere you could see its traces—leafless branches or leaves that were all reddish brown. The flames had made autumn trees of them, and to redden them further the sun beamed down the deep red of its last rays like a mordant dye.

It was six o'clock. Not a single leaf moved in the dense copse where shadows were peacefully falling unaccompanied by the slightest breeze. Then, thanks to the absolute silence of the tranquil evening, I heard a very odd noise. Try to imagine a slight, strange kind of hubbub of voices, mere sounds, sighs mixed with the beating of wings and the lapping of water that's been disturbed; a sort of babbling and agitated murmuring that you might take for the conversation of who knows what tribe possessing a mellifluous language, who had gathered you couldn't surmise where and though still invisible, you were about to run into.

"It's the noise of the lake," Vandell said. "At this hour you hear it a good ten minutes before seeing it."

The lake came into view as soon as we left the woods, stretching out before us at its broadest point (about a league). Its length was hard to tell for in the west it blended with the last discernible section of the horizon; it was motionless like a dead sea, perfectly pure and like a mirror in which were exactly duplicated the magnificent variety of reds of the setting sun. It was covered—and this was the real spectacle—by a numberless conglomeration of birds. All those birds, both known and unknown, divided into species, each with its habits, nests, cries, songs, mores, and territory, all that strange population was getting ready for the night. I could make out legions of them shifting places in the middle of the lake. They appeared as a multitude of dark marks, a sort of aquatic vegetation comparable to clumps of grass in a swamp. That was the section inhabited by duck, teal, scoter, and some diving birds which were dark in color. I recognized them even at a distance by the volumes of their heads, the way they were balanced almost on top of the water, and by the shape like little boats that aquatic birds have. Nearer by among the reeds where they trembled unseen by the thousand, coming and going, were snipe. They flew off in sudden bunches, their cry rapid, their wings bent, their dives as sudden as their departures. In the distance gray heron or Egyptian ibis passed overhead, neck outstretched, feet straight back, body made slender as a javelin. In an unprotected cove but beyond reach—a carbine could barely touch it—two big swans, that you might have taken on account of their size and beauty as a royal couple ruling over this little world, were slowly sailing along beside each other, necks curved, feathers the color of snow, a bit pink where turned toward the setting sun. At the same time battalions of starlings coming down off the hills passed above us making a noise like the wind going through poplar trees. Like an army filing by, they followed each other with a couple of seconds of interval. The entire mass soon formed just one long immense ribbon that spilled across the lake from one end to the other to melt into the fog. A moment later the noise stopped and the lake itself disappeared in a haze. Night fell. Around a hundred meters from us, a little to the right and almost at the foot of the "Tomb of the Christian Woman," I made out a knoll where five big olive trees grew. Fires were just starting to flare among the trees; it was the encampment.

eleven at night

"I REMEMBER," said Vandell that evening, "that two rifle shots' range from the seaside village of S. M—, there was a farm that for long years of my childhood represented for me the end of the world. The farm took in a group of small houses surrounded by trees, manure piles, feed, and hay. The houses were hard to see. What you saw from a distance on the slope down from the vine- yards, at the edge of the big wheat fields—a view which was de- nuded in autumn—were some old walnut trees stripped bare by the salty wind off the sea and a few rows of young elms which the farmer had pollarded. They were what made those dwellings no- ticeable, a fact that never, as far as I know, struck anyone but me. There was a close carpet of grass under the trees that birds would sometimes visit, such as huppoe, dove, and wood pigeon. What I had imagined before I was allowed to go as far as that was summed up by twin feelings, both very vague and even more confused, those of distance and the unknown. Finally the day came when some hunters whom I was accompanying took me there. It was in October and the fields were empty. Minus their twice-a-year crop the land was altogether more solemn, sonorous, and big. A bird flew out of the small grove of elm—a screech owl—and I later un- derstood, remembering that day of emancipation, that it had been in some way a beginning, the prologue to my travels. Compared to my own size, the bird that I saw flying away that day seemed to me to be something both enormous and extraordinary: its big silky wings, the delicate flight of the much-feathered thing, the all-of-a-sudden ferocious face of a bird that's been surprised. The unquiet genius of solitude, the inhospitable ideal of the unknown couldn't have appeared to me in any form resembling more the visible spirit of a chimera or assumed an aspect more imaginary as it disappeared forever. Dating from that first visit, the charm was broken and whether all the mystery of the site really vanished at the very minute I set foot there, or whether it was enough that I had grown up and adjusted my ideas of distance, things then seemed much more simple to me. Habit in the end showed me that the farmhouses resembled all other such. There was a difference, nevertheless, for the persistent memory of an illusion made them retain for me some kind of undeniable attraction."

Something akin to what he experienced happened to me his evening. The lake represented in my life as a traveler what the farm at S. M— was for the youth of Vandell: a few hundred steps to reach one and six or seven leagues at the most to get to the other, and in both cases the same constant, vague desire to see, to know, and to corroborate. Solitude made itself known when it seized the same occasion, appearing to me, in almost the same form. Perhaps it will vanish tomorrow, carried off by several thousand wings. Is the charm broken? I don't know, but it's possible. You don't bivouac out in the unknown with some thirty horses without being affected. We are staying in the encampment used by travelers coming from Cherchell or Milianah. It's near the lake at the foot of the hills and so near "Kouber-er-Roumiia" that you can see its rounded triangle outlined in shadow against the starry backdrop of the night. It lies on the highest elevation in the Sahel like the little stone pyramids that mark the long curves of the Saharan steppes. Either by land or sea you can see it from the same distance away. For fifteen centuries this old landmark has been used to guide boats and caravans, mysteriously inviting them to stop and visit. It's a small, circular plateau that the elements constantly beat down upon. It's trampled by horses, perforated by tent poles, burned by campfires, and strewn with ashes, debris, broken camp beds, everything that travelers will leave. It has a spring a stone's throw from the lake whose own water is brackish and undrinkable. These are the things along with the big olive trees, which are contemporary with whatever dynasty it is that sleeps up there under its tumulus of rocks, that make up the camp.

It's late. The moon rose around nine; it's two days from being full, not completely round, a little like a badly drawn circle, but admirably pleasing to look at, limpid and serene. Fires are lit half inside hollows at the base of the olive trees' trunks, these huge cavities acting like hearths. They've gone out except for a spark here and there. Around us remain the cold damp of October midnights, pale moonbeams, and veils of mist. No night ever provided a more sleep-inducing light or whiter hangings to shroud eyes made weary by the sun.

at the encampment by the lake,
Tuesday evening

WE SLEPT in our cold tents as you sleep when camping, in a transparent sleep that perceives things almost as distinctly as in the early evening—the noises, dim light, even the murmurs of night. Between midnight and one o'clock there was a great tumult in the camp for the horses were fighting. Three of the more high-strung ones had broken away from their stakes and after first leaping into the reeds made off toward the hills, neighing frenetically. The chase lasted two hours. Through the grayish cloth of my canvas pavilion I could see fires once again burning vigorously and I breathed in the aromatic smoke of the resinous wood. Our Arabs continued to keep watch, circled about the flames and as close as possible to the hearth so as to protect themselves from the dampness that descended as if rain, and the mosquitoes. These are two redoubtable enemies in such a season and place.

The moon went down in the mountains toward the west, and at the very moment that I lifted the tent flap, above Blidah a ruddy dawn was being born. The sky, which at first was orange, grew rapidly paler, going toward white in time with the sun as it neared the horizon. Do you remember those two fine engravings of Edwin Landseer? The values of gray and black are so completely right, it's as if they had been printed in color; one's entitled *The Sanctuary* and the other *The Challenge*. Both are singularly well observed. I couldn't offer you a better or more precise idea of the lake with the jagged silhouette of the mountains as seen at that hour of half-shadows at dawn. Then all of a sudden reveille sounded announcing the arrival of day. A few minutes later the sun, all rosy, burst out through the air that was like silver.

I said that our companions planned to turn the hunt by the lake into a massacre yet the hunt amounted to nothing at all, or almost. An obstacle no one had foreseen made the beat impossible. Boats were needed to reach the middle of the lake, and there weren't any more. The two or three little flat-bottomed tubs that hadn't sunk or filled up with mud had been taken by hunters seeking ibis who had arrived the night we did. Duck, snipe, ibis, swan, heron, all the birds that swim, or whose instinct keeps them away from the shore, were escaping our grasp. Our last resort was to go out among the reeds. Of all the ways to hunt, there is none more original or less certain. We had to take health precautions as for going swimming, and so it was noon by the time we set to hunting, in other words, took to the water.

The lake is surrounded by reeds from eight to ten feet high and so close together, disposed in thick rows as symmetrical as palisades, you'd think they had been planted on purpose so as to make access impossible. I know of no thickets harder to get through or as unpleasant to deal with. The canes bear a succession of low-water marks, muddy lines that are perfectly graduated from the the highest to the lowest point of the muck, which is the water's high point at the time. Once thrust among the packed reeds as regular as organ pipes and having sharp, cutting leaves, you can see no more than a small section of sky lying exposed directly over your head. Below you see blackish water in which you're submerged almost to the waist. It's impossible either to choose which

way to go, know where you are, or call on companions for help—
or help them—in an emergency. You have to feel your way, testing
how solid the mud is at each step to avoid bores. You must always
remain upright, holding your rifle high, with your game bag slung
high and as close to the shoulders as possible.

Vandell had taken a staff instead of a rifle and it served us as a
cane. As much as possible, we walked in each other's footsteps.
From time to time a wing would appear through the greenery or
almost brush our heads as it flew by, plunging quickly behind the
green curtain of reeds. Sometimes, you'd hear a shot at scattered
points not far away, and then thousands of ducks that you couldn't
see would take flight beating the water with their wings, sounding like a multitude of oars. I can't say how much progress we'd
made or in what section of the lake, let alone in what direction. I
know that we were conscientiously on the move from noon to five
o'clock; all that time we were cut off from the sky, hampered by
the brush and always with water at least to our hips. At the beginning we were guided by the sun, and when we could no longer see
it, by the color of the zenith. About an hour before day's end we
met up with one of the party hunting for ibis. He was set up in a
blind; the spot was bare of vegetation, a pool deep among the
reeds. It was a tiny hut on stilts. It was made of cane and had a roof
and a floor, both of which let daylight through. A boat was docked
next to it. We could only detect a rifle barrel poking out of an opening; it gave this watery citadel a rather threatening aspect. The
hunter remained motionless back in his hiding place.

"*Ya*, son of Nimrod," Vandell called to him, "hello!"

"Hello!" replied the Arab, who made himself visible, pushing
aside a patch of the hut's greenery.

"Have you had a good day?"

"Take a look in the boat," the hunter answered.

We saw three birds stretched out in the bottom of the boat: two
rather sad-colored ibis and a magnificent swan.

"He killed the king of the lake," I commented to Vandell as I looked at that beautiful bird, who'd been shot straight in the heart. The still bleeding wound make him more beautiful yet. The sun now was very low, only lighting the top of the brush; long zones of shadow spread out over the water, chilling it with their cool colors. At five-thirty we returned to the tents. Ropes were stretched between the olive trees to hang the game. I saw sultana hens, bittern, a few ducks, a small number of snipe—in all sixty-three birds.

at the encampment by the lake,
Wednesday evening

I'LL KNOW in a little bit what the results of the hunt have been, and since this letter is only supposed to be a hunter's notes, I'll add that detail to those that preceded it. We dismounted after having ridden fast for twelve hours across very beautiful country. We saw Tipaza, which resembles all the towns that have been destroyed, and the Chenoua, which with its colossal proportions, more rugged contours, and delicate iridescence, reminds you of Sainte-Baume in Provence. The Roman city is three leagues from the camp on the other side of the Sahel off at an angle toward Cherchell. Ancient Julia-Caesarea and ancient Tipaza of Caesarian Mauritania were separated by the Chenoua, which served as a common lookout for both cities. The former, now Cherchell, became Arab; Tipaza was abandoned, having been devastated and looted, destroyed from top to bottom. Only two or three things remain recognizable for anybody not an archaeologist: the gates, the roads around it, and the tombs. The tombs lie open as if the dead who had inhabited them had already been resuscitated. The lids had all been overturned, revealing empty containers that now are used as drinking troughs for horses. Sand deposited by the wind off the sea has long replaced human ashes. What's left are some inscriptions to transcribe; capitals fallen from columns and the truncated columns themselves; a rare fragment or two of marble sculpture; long sections of wall made up of narrow brick covered over by squat lentisks. There are as well two long stretches of graves that trail off into the dunes. A great quantity of white, sterile dust has long gathered on things already dead as heaps of memories. That's what left of a people who were the greatest military power, the greatest colonizer, a people responsible for architecture that was among the best engineered of any on earth. It's an example for those who neither in intellect or mores, or by the nature of what they founded, possess the solidity of Rome's genius.

We dined in the ruins where I killed two red partridges that were pecking at some seeds in the open tomb of a . . . "Hortensia . . . mourned for and missed," the inscription says by a "Tullius." I saw perched in lentisks as big as small elms whole flocks of partridge, a rare occurrence that I've yet to see elsewhere. The ropes stretched across the encampment are laden with game. It's a magnificent display of game. This evening there are 394 partridges, rabbits, and hares.

Blidah, end of October

Two DAYS after our return from the lake Vandell and I went back to exploring the plain. It was *sebt* (Saturday) and market day for the Hadjout. As we were leaving the market we noted festivities in progress, and we received from the caid himself a formal note inviting us to the *diffa* that evening.

The festivities were a sort of cantonal get-together organized by several neighboring *douars* sharing expenses in order to have a good time riding, racing, and shooting. These are the last remaining pleasures of that small tribe which has lost three-quarters of its members. They are deprived of the real pleasures of military life for peace bores as if so much nothingness. The Hadjout have never liked nor practiced anything but warlike pursuits. You became a Hadjout the way you became a soldier. As for the women-folk—wives or mothers, daughters or sisters of soldiers—their martial pleasure was to saddle the horses that were going off to war, arm with their own hands their intrepid men, observe them from a distance, welcome them back with ululating enthusiasm, bandage wounds bravely received, and cry over the dead. This was their part in an adventurous existence of which war in all its forms, small and great, constituted its foundation, motive, charm, and profit. That's why a fantasia, which isn't as good as war but has a resemblance, is the spectacle today best able to console those veterans who no longer engage in it and the young people who never did.

"You'll find nothing there," Vandell had told me, "that you haven't already known for a long time: people gathering under some tents, a show of horseback riding followed by nighttime dances and an epic repast. But it is a gesture of politeness that's owed the caid who's expecting us. Furthermore, perhaps we'll enjoy ourselves for I've lots of friends among the Hadjout, beginning with that rogue of an Amar-ben-Arif, who will show off to you his tricks in juggling and horsemanship.

As it turned out, my friend, Amar-ben-Arif was to be the day's principal figure, and in a much more serious way than imagined by Vandell. He had in store for us as surprises a tragic exploit and a dreadful loss.

Noon found us at the marketplace, where we knew we would see the caid and so pay him the double honor of coming to his audience at the *sebt* and greeting him directly in his tent. The *sebt* is held at the far end of the plain on Hadjout land, which is part of the moors extending from Mouzïa to the lake. As you know by its name, it takes place on the seventh day of the week, presided over by an officer from the Office for Arab Affairs or the caid. The latter serves as judge during days that are packed with various disputes, disagreements over rights, and accusations of cheating, all being small judicial matters that can't be kept out of any human intercourse. They get settled on the spot.

An Arab market resembles one of our village fairs. You see the same behavior, or just about, and the same participants—country folk, itinerant peddlers, hawkers, and horse dealers. Only change the nationality and substitute *chaouchs* armed with sticks and the mounted *beylik* for our rural police and gendarmes and the folding tent of the caid for the city hall. Imagine African rather than French food; herds of camels injecting their physiognomies and groans of complaint, which have nothing analogous; enclosures of animals, comprising goats, sheep, donkeys, mules, horses, and skinny cows and you begin to have an idea of what the *sebt* is like. It's left to you to imagine the grandeur of the site. There's the breadth of the surrounding plain, the beauty that goes with the horizons of the Mitidja, the solemnity of the Algerian moors, the brilliance of light, and the harshness of the sun, which is unbearable even in October. Finally, you'll see assembled tents with the conic shape of pavilions used for travel or war, an interesting symbol, which is the expression of the mores of a primitive society. In Europe, however, tents are an absurd custom and always suspect. They're the dwellings of people without any real occupation, within which are found wanderers presumed not to have either hearth or fixed address. The nomad there is more or less a vagabond. And to get even closer to reality, you must imagine the particular murmurings of Arab crowds, the novelty of dress—everyone practically the same, almost all in white—and, last, certain local trades that appear strange being so extremely rudimentary.

The butchers arrive dangling a selection of bleeding carcasses. There are blacksmiths, cobblers, preparers of coffee, men who roast meat, all with their tools and equipment of the simplest; people from the south with their wool and dates; those from the plain with grain and mountain folk with oil, firewood as well as charcoal. The farmers from Blidah bring every fruit and vegetable that can be cultivated from oranges to citrons, including roasted chickpeas (the parched kernels of the Bible) and lentils. They make with the latter a reddish-brown soup in memory of Esau's dish. The Jewish and Arab peddlers sell notions, medicines, essences, crude jewelry, cottons from everywhere as well as all kinds of other cloth, etc. Each has his own stall either covered or open to the winds and in both cases they are arranged most simply. One or two boxes, or instead, baskets to contain the merchandise, a mat for showing them, a length of cloth as parasol is about what's needed in the way of accoutrements for the itinerant merchant.

The arrangements of the artisans are scarcely more complicated. The blacksmith, whom I'll take as example, is a man dressed in travel garb, wearing a veil and a jacket, his feet covered with woven leather sandals. He carries with him in the hood of his cloak all the instruments of a trade that resembles a fantasy art, so few are the opportunities he has to exercise it. This means bits of worked or unworked iron, a hammer, nails, a reed pipe, a very modest supply of charcoal, and, not least, the anvil, which is actually a portable instrument resembling a hammer and whose handle is used as shank and fulcrum. If, let's say, he finds a horse to shoe as soon as he arrives, he does the following: he makes a hole in the ground and prepares the forge's fire; he sets his anvil next to the forge, squatting so as to hold it between his knees, and selects some iron from his stock. He's then ready to start work. An apprentice, a neighbor, or the first person to pass, offers the artisan his help in blowing on the fire, kindly lending him his lungs. Once the iron is hot and shaped, all the rest is done as in Europe but with less effort and care, above all with less finish. Rarely is a horseshoe anything more than a sort of very thin crescent, half eaten through by rust, resembling leather that's been cut from an old boot no longer of any use. When charcoal is lacking, it gets replaced with peat, or simpler yet, with camel dung that burns readily and slowly with a little sputtering sound like a cigar. It's immediately recognizable by its fetid combination of odors.

Stands, buyers, merchants, people on foot and on horseback, beasts of burden and animals for sale are all found cheek by jowl without much thought for order or safety. Large dromedaries walk about freely, making a path for themselves like giants in a group of dwarfs. Livestock circulate wherever they can, and a donkey that's staked fraternizes with one that's for sale. In this confusion only those directly involved can maintain their bearings, and it's hard to distinguish buyers from sellers. Business is conducted in a low voice with country ruses and an Arab dealer's wheedlings. They smoke a pipe or two to help deliberations, they drink coffee as a friendly way to reach an agreement; and then there is, as in France, a meaningful handshake to seal the bargain just concluded. Payment is made reluctantly, money being counted out slowly and painfully as if life's blood. Yet concealed in a handkerchief (here that ordinarily serves as the moneybag) you can hear it clinking long before it decides to show its face. That mysterious thing that's so carefully shielded, so well defended and hidden, is called *douro*.

In the center of this temporary encampment is the caid's tent topped by the three copper balls and crescent.[28] In front is the tricolor Arab Office standard that accompanies a military chief everywhere. Two beautiful, fully saddled horses stood hobbled by its entrance. Inside there were rugs, cushions, and arms deposited in corners. A broad straw hat along with a pretty, engraved silver cup hanging from a long rope of red silk with gold tassels were hitched to the tent pole. Such, my friend, is the usual war tent. This one, in addition, resembled a court of law. Its clients, who all had moneybags, were concerned with finding a spot and all were talking about the burning issue of the instant—debts, shortfalls, errors, various quarrels over money. The caid was in the center to the rear giving orders, dispatching *chaouch*, and from time to time himself accepting, counting with his own hands some sort of tax. It was paid with copper coins that went straight into a big pouch with a gold-colored bottom that I had first thought was for tobacco. He's a man of forty-five at least, very tall, very thin, very handsome with the bored look fitting someone in command. He had much dignity in his ways, a ruddy and yellowish complexion, and a physiognomy both imperious and gentle. He was dressed in white like an Old Testament priest; he wore no burnoose but had a veil around his head and was wrapped in a *haik* over his summer *gandoura*. He was impeccably dressed yet informal in style in those white garments of his—a great lord in his house clothes. He was affable with Vandell and polite with me. He wasn't aware of exactly what either one of us was doing in his territory, one with his pen and barometer and me with my box of colors and drawing pencils. He did recognize that a man can wish to learn and that there's much to learn in the place where he himself lived. Furthermore, as long as you're not like everybody else, have no known trade, and are not a *mercanti,* as they say, they are curious about your activities, and in such cases a stranger always has an easy time among the Arabs. Everything that's put down in writing on paper in their eyes is of general interest. And why couldn't a painter be a political spy? Politics is basic in their life, as well as in their hopes and suspicions.

When the moment came to close the session, the caid had his horse brought. His horsemen mounted, his musicians in a group lined up behind him. Following custom, the standard-bearer placed himself between the caid and the musicians. I assumed that entourage, seeming quite superfluous, had no other purpose that to reflect prestige. And so to the steady sound of drums, hautboys, and flutes and keeping the dignified pace of a procession, we completed the short distance that separated us from the appointed meeting place at the festivities.

It wasn't far from the *douars,* on land that was uncultivated but with little vegetation, chosen expressly to make racing easy. On one side open tents had been set up for guests who might wish to rest and on the other a big tent of dark-colored wool, as vast as a house, entirely enclosed except for one spot that looked out on the empty horizon. The panel that faced the race course had been lowered all the way to the ground; however, since the cloth was old and riddled with holes, the women (it was their tent) had more than enough windows through which to see out, but none of them being big enough for them to be seen. Outside a bunch of children were frolicking like chicks on the edge of a barnyard; two or three watchdogs guarded the approaches.

Exactly across from the women's tent, above which flew a small red flag, the silk standard of the caid was planted. Those two banners indicated the width of the hippodrome, which lengthwise stretched out indefinitely, as well as the end of the track for the racers. The well-disciplined horses were supposed to come up short when they reached this goal where rifles are fired and greetings of gunpowder are addressed first to the right and the caid, then to the women on the left.

It was four o'clock and the preparations seemed about completed. The *diffa* was cooking in the enclosed tent where a hubbub could be heard. The preparations released a strong odor of stew mixed with smoke from green wood as if from a kitchen's basement windows. Rhythmic singing and the clapping of hands gave out the slow and monotonous beat of a traditional dance (a lesser and more decent version of the Egyptian "dance of the bee"). At intervals bursts of unbridled joy covered the swawks of chickens struggling under a servant's knife. Every horseman worthy of the name in Hadjout territory had gathered: a dense row of around two hundred horses blocked the southern limits of the race course. The encampment was filling with men in war gear, coming and going in the field with the hesitant walk that the size and weight that two layers of footwear and, above all, the long dragging spurs lend to Arab horsemen.

Just now a small cavalcade made up of just two mules, each mounted by a woman in city garb and copiously veiled, arrived out of the plain from the direction of Blidah. A black preceded them, riding a donkey sidesaddle; a black woman accompanied them on foot.

"There's Assra and Saïd," said Vandell, recognizing Hawa's servant and her husband.

"In that case," I said, "it's not hard to presume who the two women riders are."

They entered the camp but didn't dismount where the women stay. Instead, they were made to cross through the whole crowd. Someone from among the organizers of the festivities led them straight to a little tent that had been set up off to one side. In it were rugs and cushions, giving all appearance of having been readied for an expected guest to stay in privacy. Incidentally, no one took any special notice of their arrival; I heard someone near me suggest that they were dancers.

As soon as they were installed, one of them removed her veil: the beautiful Aichouna could be seen in that light, transparent style of dress she favors and that so becomes her. The other just opened her *haik* sufficiently for us to recognize her. We could tell that she was elegantly gotten up, having around her neck in addition to her necklaces and other jewelry at least twelve ells of strung flowers.

"You would have done better to have stayed at home," Vandell told her.

Without replying, Hawa made a gesture of indifference implying that everything was more or less the same to her; she had no particular reason for coming here but also none for being bored. I saw her smile that inexpressible smile that was such a great part of her grace as well as her coldness. She smiled as if at the sad fate that already seemed to have been decided for her.

The caid didn't go near the tent nor did any of the older or more serious among the men. A space was left all around it less out of discretion than disdain. You only noticed some young men of around sixteen to twenty milling about a few feet away from the opened tent flap. They had an indolent air, an annoying manner, and bony, chalky, wan faces, their eyes lined with black. They wore their hats a little to one side. They smiled at the radiant Aichouna, who seemed to be known to all. They also looked at—it was within their rights—yet in this case with a certain embarrassment mixed with impertinence, the small woman with the serious way of carrying herself. None of them appeared to know her.

"Are they going to remain there," I asked Vandell, "away from the other women, like entertainers or low-caste Indians? They're exposed—in broad daylight yet—to the curiosity of a troop of soldiers as well as to the scrutiny of their handsome sons whose looks can only dishonor them."

"What can be done about prejudice?" Vandell said. "It's all around us and neither you nor I will change anything. No, my friend, Hawa won't be admitted to the tent of married women with families. There they speak a language that she has perhaps never spoken and where they take part in games that would make her pale cheeks blush. One has shown her face, the others remain veiled; one receives at home, the others keep the door shut. It isn't a matter of feelings, it's a question of order. The entire difference resides in a curtain: lowered and the woman's honest; raised and she no longer is. As you can see, it's a fiction and quite unreasonable; it is, however, sacred as a principle and worthy of respect as far as duty is concerned. Furthermore," Vandell added, "let prejudice take its course. It's hypocritical, unjust, and cruel; it makes victims, choosing them badly and sacrificing them without having the right. But at bottom, it's useful. Intolerance is the hypocrisy of virtue, of that I'm in agreement; but it's also the last homage rendered the moral law by a people no longer possessing morals."

Just as the starting shots for the race were heard, Aichouna said to her friend, "Come, the horses are taking off."

"Good-bye," said Hawa and I returned her "good-bye" as usual. It could have been "farewell" for I'd only see her again once back in her tent, half-dead and unrecognizable.

We first witnessed servants and dependents racing, people of the lower class, who were the most poorly mounted of the tribe. They were shabby, riders without any style mounted on small horses. They had old rusty rifles and their horses had only a piece of string for bridle. Riders like this can catch anyone's interest only if they're fast. They ride their horses as if they were fleet birds, not guiding them at all, hardly controlling them, letting them gallop with a lightness that made no more noise than the beating of wings. The first horse to come along will do, even if only half-trained or maybe too young to compete; it just has to look lively, and the meanest of weapons is all right as long as it has powder and will go off without exploding. When they have neither boots nor spurs, they made do with a switch and the sharp edge of the stirrup; not having a crop, they cry out *"Arrach!"* That sound has a kind of irresistible resonance for their horses that are as excitable as they are docile. There's no question of making a show or displaying equestrian skills; it's enough to run flat out, fire off your gun upon reaching the goal, and pass by the tent where the women are, take in their ululations, which correspond in the way of applause to the salvos of the muskets that had saluted them. In such a situation these most aristocratic of all people on earth are full of bonhomie. Everyone has as good time as he can; the valet races next to his master, that is, if his horse is fast enough to keep up with him. The principle applied to military games comes into play: before the enemy there is no distinction of caste, no superiority by birth, one rider being the equal of another, a horse's gallop making all stations in life the same.

This prelude was very brief, lasting only a few minutes; it baited the spectators and let the horses sniff the odor of gun powder. The caid had taken his place by the flag with near him his two sons, pretty boys of six and ten. The elder one had the dress, boots, and haircut of a young soldier, wearing long leggings of yellow leather. He lorded it like a young prince as if the spectacle were given in his honor. So as to be more comfortable, he leaned back on two gray-bearded servants, who, lying prone, acted as cushions. Cries went up from the end of the racing field where the cavalry, which was about to take part, practiced in small platoons.

The first group was magnificent; twelve to fifteen riders burst forth in a line. These were the elite, both men and horses. The mounts were in parade harness; the men in holiday gear, meaning combat attire: voluminous pantaloons, *haik* twisted around as a scarf, wide belts fitted with cartridges and fastened very high across sleeveless, vividly colored vests. Having taken off together, they reached the destination in a solid line—which is rare with the Arabs—boots meeting, stirrup against stirrup, high in the saddle, arms outstretched, reins to the wind, letting out yells, and making broad gestures. All the same, they had such perfect equilibrium that most of them carried their rifles balanced on headgear resembling turbans, and with both hands now free, brandished either a pistol or saber. All the rifles were waving above our heads just ten feet away from us in a way that can't be described; one second later each man was motionless, taking aim before us. The sun sparkled on the arms, the baldrics of the swords, the gold jewelry; and we saw in rapid flashes cloth, embroidered saddles, stirrups and bridles decorated with gold glitter. They passed by like lightning in a general discharging of all rifles; we were covered with powder and enveloped in white smoke. The women applauded. A second platoon followed right behind so that the smoke of the firing of these rifles blended with the first. The second discharge acted as an almost instantaneous echo. Following in their traces was yet a third group in a new whirlwind of dust, their rifles pointing toward the ground. It was led by a black man named Kaddour who was famous in the plain for his phenomenal gray mare. She's a little flat-sided beast, very limber and graceful. Mouse-colored, she's completely shaved, that is, without mane and with a hairless tail resembling the flag of a hound. Tarnished silver ornaments, bells, amulets, a multitude of dangling little chains embellished her with an original get-up full of rustling noises and flashing reflections. Kaddour was in a scarlet vest and purple pants. He carried two rifles, one on his head, the other in his left hand. In his right he had a pistol that he fired off; he then discharged his two rifles, one after the other. He changed hands, tossing them as a juggler who manages two sticks, and then disappeared stretched across the neck of his beast, his chin resting on what should have been her mane.

There was no letting up in the discharge of rifles. Shot after shot nonstop, the riders came in waves through a curtain of dust and gunpowder; the women, who continued clapping and giving out their bizarre yelps, could for one hour breathe the exciting atmosphere of a battlefield. Try to imagine the things that can never be reborn in these notes with their cold form and trailing sentences. Imagine the impetuous actions amid disorder and those things that almost elude you because of their speed, all this set in brilliant, harshly colored relief as the sun beats down. Picture for yourself the glitter of arms; the flashing light off all those groups in movement; the *haiks* loosened in the race and the rippling of the wind through cloth; the radiance, as fleeting as a flash of lightning, of so many shining things—the bright reds, oranges the color of fire, cold whites submerged in the grays in the sky. Just picture the velvet saddles—those of gold thread; the pompoms on the headstalls of the horses; their golden blinders, breastplates, and bridles; their bits, whose straps are covered in sweat, dripping with foam. Added to this excess of delight provided the eyes, an even more stupefying tumult meant for the ears followed. We heard the cries of the riders, the screams of the women, the din of the guns, the awesome galloping of the horses as they burst forward at top speed, the ringing—the rattling—of thousands and thousands of sounding things. Now return the site to the way it really is, and which you know well, that's calm, yellowish tan, and somewhat coated with dust. Then perhaps you'll make out in this confusion of joyous activity and festivity, actually as intoxicating as war, the stunning spectacle that's called a fantasia, a spectacle waiting to be painted. One man alone today could understand it and know how to interpret it; he alone would have the fantasy, ingenuity as well as the power, the audacity—the right—to try it.

Break down the fantasia into its rather simple components. In that profusion of display find one group and in that group, one rider: it's a galloping horse being well ridden. It's still a unique spectacle, as is any equestrian exercise that shows us a moment of common action and mutual agreement by the two most intelligent and perfectly formed creatures that God created. When separated, the two alone appear to us to be incomplete for neither one nor the other has his maximum strength. Combine them by blending man with horse, give the torso initiative and will, allowing the rest of the body the combined attributes of alacrity and vigor, and you have a being that's supremely strong, intelligent and active, courageous and fleet, free yet under control. The artists of Greece never conceived anything more natural or greater. They were able to demonstrate that an equestrian statue is the ultimate in rendering man in sculpture. Out of this monster that has life-size proportions, being an audacious figurative union of a robust horse and a handsome man, they created the teacher of Greece's heroes. He was the inventor of the sciences and the preceptor of the most agile, bravest, and handsome of its men.[29]

From time to time, like first-class performers who are quite sure of themselves and know they will always receive applause, some riders raced either alone or two by two. In the latter case, the combination of two horses appeared to be controlled by one hand or tied to one invisible shaft. These riders are worth mentioning: there was Kaddour, who rejoined the race with that mare of his built like a greyhound; Djelloul, on a dark bay covered in dark red silk; Ben-Said-Khrelili, dressed in pink and riding a horse that was all black like a crow; and one-armed Mohammed-ben-Daoud. They passed the loaded rifles to this aged survivor of other wars, who being unable to shoulder them fired them like pistols with one arm extended. Old Bou-Noua, brother-in-law of the caid, participated, accompanied by just his three sons, charming youths in simple attire who acted as his pages. He rode a tall horse that was heavily accoutered and thickly shoed; it had a broad neck and chest and galloped ponderously like a horse in a Rubens with hocks bent back, the repetitive curves of its muscles bulging, and its hooves thundering. He himself was enormous—tall, big with a big belly, a fan-shaped beard, fair in complexion, eyes quite round and light in color like those of an eagle. He wore a singularly voluminous, floating *haik* that as he raced along seemed to fly. In addition to a sword with a gold baldric he had two or three vests all worked in gold forming around his torso a sort of breastplate off which the sun shone as if it were indeed armor. He didn't stand when he galloped since the weight of his dress and his own embonpoint prevented him from attaining complete upright but was somewhat elevated in the stirrups, one hand squarely on the pommel, the other waving a long rifle, a magnificent firearm that he disdained to charge with gunpowder. A Kabyle saber in a silver scabbard hanging from his left shoulder completed his splendid war gear. After every race they took part in, the riders went back at a walk, though some charged as vigorously as ever. They would stop for a moment in the middle of the field, making their horses rear so as to excite them further, smacking them with the bridle, spurring them while they were stationary. Parading their beasts, they'd then return to the starting point, to form a battle formation once more.

In the middle of this extravagance, disorder, and noise the adventurous Amar-ben-Arif passed to and fro. I hadn't seen him since the evening at Hassan's. I remembered the chess player who had been sober of gesture and sparing with words. When Vandell told me, "There's Ben-Arif," I no longer recognized him.

On horseback he appeared to me to be short, less elegant than many others but for solidity having no equal. You could feel that he was unshakable, and whether he was out of the saddle or clinging to it, standing or seated, even when dangerously off balance, he was in control of his massive strength, having a wrestler's facility in switching positions. You could see only the upper portion of his cheeks, which were of a white-hot pallor, the two bristling pointed ends of his mustache and his eyes, which were the color of coals just aglow. Modestly dressed in dark-colored material with much embroidery, he had all sorts of firearms tucked in his belt. He managed his grayish stallion like a consummate horseman; its harness, which was half violet leather and half metal, resembled chased steel. For a rifle he had a double-barreled French weapon into which he poured handfuls of powder, loading it on the run. We saw him at scattered intervals, alone or accompanied, yet always recognizable by the somewhat odd look on his face, his horse's coat with its bluish steel reflections and the double retort of his gun that would go off right in front of us. His presence was also known by the loudness of his gallop since, contrary to the nearly general custom among the tribesmen, his horse was shod.

"*Ya,* Ben-Arif!" they yelled at him, "careful with your horse, he's bleeding! You'll cut him straight through to the guts if you don't watch out!"

He answered simply, "Don't worry, I have another."

And off he took, flat out, exhibiting a kind of gallop that, if not faster, was at least much more impetuous than that of the others.

At last, not out of lassitude but undoubtedly out of pity for his mount, or out of precaution, as we were to understand later, he stopped. He examined the flanks of his beast where each jab of a spur given with an especially hard kick was outlined by a border of bristling hairs, a line of reddish flesh, and a trickle of blood. He stanched the wounds with a little grass, and with soil mixed with saliva he plugged the wounds that were bleeding a lot. He rapidly sponged with a corner of his *haik* wherever the horse was foamed up, loosening its harness slightly to ease the gasping for breath. In a singular compliment he planted a kiss on its nostrils, calling it by a name that I couldn't hear. He then leaped on the substitute horse that a stable boy has holding. It was a stallion, a bay going toward cherry-red, fresh and well-rested and already all done up as if for a war expedition. A long *djebira* hung from the pommel of the saddle. We could see tucked under the girth a Spanish-made saber with a slightly curved blade and without any scabbard, its hilt of horn.

"That madman will end up by committing some foolishness," Vandell observed as he watched him flying away.

Amar-ben-Arif reappeared after a few minutes and as he passed in front of us, greeted us by firing twice at point-blank range. The caid made a sign to him and said, "Wait a bit, Ben-Arif, I'm going to ride."

Night was approaching, the festivities were about to end, and I was therefore surprised that the caid had waited this long to take part.

He kept on his babouches and just buckled his belt, lifting up the skirts of his long *haik* that covered him loosely and gave him a kind of youthful and haughty elegance, so as to be freer in his movements. He mounted his white horse, the same one that had brought him to the market. Three young men who hadn't yet ridden followed his example. They slowly took to the field, then stopped. Amar was on his left, a young man who was a nephew on his right—in all five horsemen. I heard the caid say to his companions, "Are you ready?" And simultaneously the five horsemen began to ride. They arrived abreast and in starting order. The caid wasn't armed. Three rifles went off: it was the three young men. Amar didn't fire. Quickly, he laid his rifle across the saddle and reined in his horse as if he were going to make it jump. Instead, the animal lunged to the left. As it was only a couple of feet away from the spectators, after lifting itself straight up, it fell square among them with all four feet. There was an agonizing cry—as I write I can still hear it—then yelling, then an uproar. The crowd parted and I saw on the ground something in white that rolled about, then lay still.

"Ah, the wretch!" exclaimed Vandell.

"Seize him!" bellowed the caid, who threw himself at Amar.

But no one was quick enough to grab him and he passed near us almost knocking us over. Turning to see who was following him, he gave a loud whistle. His first horse, as exhausted as it was, slipped out of the hands of the groom and took off like a shot. A few seconds later we saw a small group of riders riding full tilt across the plain in a cloud of dust. A short distance ahead, no more than a pistol shot away, you could make out Ben-Arif, lying almost flat in the saddle, heading straight for the mountain, and near him his relief horse with empty saddle, galloping with the easeful gait of a wild horse.

This tragic accident happened so quickly that I saw at the very same moment—you really could say in the batting of an eyelash —the shying of the horse, the flight of Amar, and then the uproar of the people who rushed to the side of the person who had been struck. I also heard the chorus of confused cries, "The wretch— stop him—hurry!" and the voices of the crowd saying, "The woman's dead!"

I looked at Vandell. He had understood my gesture. He said to me, "Yes . . . it's her."

Yes, it was poor Hawa who had received the full impact of Amar's horse, straight on, right in the face. She was not yet dead but she had by her right eyebrow a gaping wound exposing her skull. She was bleeding copiously and was soaked from head to toe. Quite unconscious and hollow-eyed, her features marked by a horrible pallor, she moaned feebly. They carried her into the little tent and placed her on a mattress. Immediately, they ran to the kitchen to prepare red-hot irons to cauterize her wounds, which is the Arab way of treating them; but the caid and Vandell, who both examined her, said, each in turn, that it was useless.

At the end of an hour she regained consciousness. She looked about, that beautiful eye of hers that had received the blow looking at us as if through a veil of blood.

"Ya, habibi," she said to me. "Oh, my friend, I've been killed," and trying again to make herself understood, "He killed me!"

A crowd was gathering about the wounded woman and groups of the curious were commenting in emotional tones on the accident. In no one's eyes did it pass as an act of clumsiness on Ben-Arif's part.

"He killed her, really and truly," Vandell said to me. "He wanted to. Perhaps he'd wanted to for a long time . . . she was his wife . . . that's what they're saying, and if we had been more curious, we would have known it sooner. He killed her first husband so as to marry her, and she left him after learning that he was the assassin. And today he has assassinated her, proving that murder does not weigh very heavily when desire or hatred is involved."

It was just about six o'clock; the festivities had ended; night was descending—a black curtain falling on this drama.

I took hardly any part, my friend, in what ensued and the remainder of that doleful watch-keeping can be told in a few words. As soon as night had fallen, all the while the wounded woman was in death's throes with Aichouna in attendance watching her die, along with Assra, who wept, the *diffa* was served and everyone went to partake of it. For an hour or two I could only hear the low murmuring of the crowd at their repast, which was eaten on the grass, and the coming and going of the cooks serving the dishes. Then after the *diffa* came the dances. A young man, a boy of sixteen, was chosen to replace Aichouna. She was the one most missed of the two absent women. They set bonfires on the moors, huge fires of brushwood that spread light from high in the sky. A big circle was formed, reaching from the women's tent almost to Hawa's pavilion, which nobody went near anymore. Two or three candles dimly illuminated with their trembling light the shadowy figures of the two crying women bent over and almost covering the unconscious body of the dying person.

Nevertheless, the dancer began, slowly at first, to go around the circle in front of the spectators; he stopped in front of each group in turn. He would halt and perform, accompanied tirelessly by the voices of the singers and by the monotonous clapping of hands, the identical, unvarying pantomime. Each person, in return for this treat that was always the same, held out a small coin, which the dancer accepted on either his forehead or on a cheek. He continued taking the contributions until his face was nearly covered with coins.

Between eleven o'clock and midnight, the horsemen returned, exhausted from a four-hour chase. They didn't bring back Ben-Arif, who had escaped through a mountain pass.

The night was magnificent with stars yet extremely damp and cold. We remained seated on the grass until morning, shivering in the dew. The dancer had grown tired and danced no more; the supply of songs exhausted, the singing broke off; the fires continued sputtering in the midst of absolute silence; people were crouched down, at least three-quarters of them nodding off.

As deep repose spread over the valley, toward four o'clock we entered the tent for the last time. A candle stub was going out. Aichouna was sleeping. Assra, overwhelmed by fatigue, her hair in disorder and her face scored by her own fingernails, had out of exhaustion let herself fall off to sleep. Hawa was dead. Her head a bit to one side, her arms stretched out stiffly, eyelids closed, deep in an unending sleep. She was just about the way we had been used to seeing her asleep on her silken platform, and she was still covered with those white flowers of hers, which this time survived her.

Blidah, end of October

HERE I am, my friend, alone this time. Vandell has left me. We parted this very day. He left for I'm not exactly sure where, or why. He went off because the season warned him to take to the road, it being his destiny to live on the open road and to die there, so he says, when his time has come.

He'd announced his decision three days ago. He gathered up everything in his room, including collections, documents, and notes, and carried them somewhere else. He laid in a fresh supply of tobacco, the one thing that he sometimes misses when he's in the middle of the desert, and at six this morning was ready.

"If you'd care to," he said, "we can go up toward where the Ben-Moussa stay, stopping either where the telegraph is or in the cedar wood. We could then say good-bye up there on the mountain, delaying the moment as long as possible."

I mounted my horse to accompany him.

Many people from the tribes recognized him as we crossed the market square: "Good morning, Sidi-bou-Djaba," they said. "Where are you going?"

"I'm leaving."

"You're leaving Blidah?"

"Yes."

"Will you pass through . . . ?" and each named his tribe's territory.

"Perhaps," Vandell answered, "if it so pleases God."

"Have a good trip, Sidi-bou-Djaba, and may God protect you, may peace accompany you and may your way be safe!"

"Peace be to you all!" Vandell replied. "In the spring I'll be going where your people are."

To one he said, "end of December," to another, "when the snows have gone," and yet to others, "in the rainy season," all according to how he intended to use the different portions of the coming winter. Just as we were crossing the entrance to the ravine, a thought came to him all of a sudden. He said, "Do you know, it's just eight months that I passed through here, thinking that I would come to Blidah for eight days?"

You know, my friend, the steep road that we took, that long ramp of corkscrew turns that begins in the bed of the river, making big circles on the mountain's north side? After four or five hours of riding it takes you to the summit that's directly over Blidah. About halfway up is the ice house where they're were some Maltese who supplied snow. There were also some burners of charcoal and hunters. One or two buildings, now serving as shelters, are left. They stand on the edge of the narrow esplanade, and there on a clear March morning—it's too many years ago for me to remember just how many—the two of us saw eagles flying. We picked flowers; they aren't in bloom now since it's autumn. A little higher, on a peak visible from Blidah perches the telegraph with its long, articulated arms that during the days of thick winter fog could be a corpse's. An old marabout survives at the very top among the cedars in the mountain's remaining peaceful refuge. It's shaped like a sugar loaf. It used to be open but these days is barricaded by brush; it's not in ruins even though it looks totally abandoned. The flat area at the summit isn't a hundred paces in diameter; it's surrounded by cedars and covered with flat, white, unhewn rock that has been so vigorously scrubbed by precipitation then blasted by the sun to have taken on the look of dry, barren bones that have long lain in the open air. Coarse, short grass with a metallic look, the only kind that can grow in this stony soil given the harshness of the mountain climate, along with grayish lichen and bits of some kind of spiny moss unknown to me make up the impoverished, forlorn covering of that rocky place. The cedar trees are short but very broad; their leaves are blackish and their trunks are the color of rusted iron. The wind, snow, rain, and sun seem even more punishing here than in the plains. Then there's lightning that from time to time strikes the cedars and splits them in two as with a supernatural blow from an ax. All the bad weather from the worst every season has to offer inflicts on them mortal wounds and yet doesn't cause them to die. They shed their covering of needles that then carpet the area around their trunks. Passersby cut off branches, shepherds mutilate them, woodsmen get firewood from them. Bit by bit they meet their end, yet intrepidly as with all stout things. Their roots are as solid as the stone that nourishes them, the sap—maybe fleeing from the inevitable fate of certain death —takes refuge in the strong branches that still grow green and produce cones.

We sat down at the foot of these worthy old trees full of good counsel. We had a beautiful day but it seemed sad to me, and neither one or us was feeling joyous. It was warm and still. It was an occasion I'll never forget. I owe to it the strongest impression of grandeur and sense of complete peace that you can experience. The silence was so extreme, the air so motionless that we noticed the sound of our words and involuntarily we lowered our voices.

The horizon forms a perfect circle, except for one point where the blackish cone of the Mouzaïa sticks out, as plotted from the spot I mentioned that's by the marabout. To the north, we took in the plain, its villages hardly noticeable, its roads traced in pale lines, then all the Sahel, extending from Algiers like a roll of dark cloth, its exact location being determined by its white houses. Those houses led us to the Chenoua whose base thrusts out in a distinctive way, like a promontory between two inlets; beyond, between the African coast and the sky's infinity, the sea stretched as far as you could see like a blue desert. In the southeast we could make out the Djurdjura, which is always whitish; in the opposite direction the dark pyramid of Ouarensenis. Eighty leagues of air belonging to no one, cloudless and without a blemish, separated those two military outposts placed at the extremities of Kaybilia.

Fifteen leagues of mountains staggered in ranks that were impossible to read, crisscrossing each other—drowned, blended in a network of indefinable tones of azure—lay at our feet. We should have been able to see Médéah if the town weren't hidden by the Nador, lost as it is in the bend of a ravine which itself is the downside of a very high plateau where it can snow. Full south and well beyond this vague arrangement of round shapes and folds, of valleys and heights—geographically, it's a panoramic map of the vast mountainous region which we call the Tell and the Atlas—we could perceive tracings that were blurred, with almost no curve, stretched out like bluish wires between elevated outcroppings, the last of which, on the right, is home to the citadel of Boghar. Yet farther south the horizon is flattened indicating where the plains begin. And last, at the very end of that interminable expanse, in a kind of ill-defined mirage in which the earth has neither solidity nor color and where the eye is overwhelmed, ready to take mountains for lengths of gray vapor, I saw—or at least Vandell named them with the assurance of a well-traveled geographer—the seven heads of Seba-Rous, and as expected, the defile of Guelt-Esthel and the gateway to Ouled-Nayl territory. Half of French Africa[30] stretched before us: the eastern Kabyles, those to the west, the Algiers massif, the Atlas, the steppes, and directly across from the sea, the Sahara.

"There's my territory," Vandell said to me. "The world belongs to the man who travels."

And he stretched his arms out in a sweeping gesture that seemed to hold for a moment the whole visible perimeter of that African land that he had made his mind's property.

For a few minutes, he focused on a white point to the north that seemed to float between the indeterminate sky and the very pale sea.

"It's a ship returning to France," I told him.

He squinted hard to lessen the brilliance of the light that was blinding us, and said, "Maybe. I've sometimes seen them from even farther away."

Then he turned his back to the sea and didn't look at it again.

"Do you think that we will see each other again?" I asked him.

"That depends on you. Yes, if you come back here; no, if I have to go to France where I probably will never go. What would I do there? I'm no longer one of your kind. After having dispensed my civilization all about me," he added, smiling, "I don't have sufficient left me to live over there where—so they say—you have too much."

As night drew near, Vandell checked the height of the sun and got up.

"It's four o'clock or around there," he said. "Leave now. You have just enough time to slip and slide down to the source of the river, and taking the ravine return home at a trot. I just have a short way to go, two leagues of gentle incline and I'll have found a *douar.*"

Upon which he whistled to his mare who came of her own accord, out of long habit presenting the proper flank for him to mount. Settled in that saddle of his formed like an armchair, he lit his pipe, just sitting without moving for a minute, without smoking or looking at anything. Suddenly, he held out his brown, bony hand to me, saying, "Who knows? *Insha Allah*, if it pleases God! That's the final word—the sum of human wisdom."

Almost immediately, he started descending the trail, leaning well back in the saddle to give some relief to his beast whose forelegs were straining because of the very steep pitch.

"Good luck!" he yelled once more.

Then, as if a happy memory had come to mind, he stopped his mare and added, "Remember this, and it's not from me. It's our jovial friend Ben-Hamida speaking: 'When you act try to use happiness rather than a hundred horsemen.'"

"Farewell," I said a last time, holding out my hands toward him, already a distance away.

Then he turned around and disappeared. Five minutes later I neither heard nor saw anything more. A light wind, the first breath of air since noon, made a couple of cones fall from the cedars. They rolled down the slope, plummeting down the trail that Vandell had taken. I looked toward the south which was where he was going, then at the trail to the north that I would take to go down.

"Sid-Bou-Djaba has left?" the Arab who accompanied me asked, as he held the stirrup.

"Yes," I answered.

"And you? Where are you going?"

"Oh, I'm going to Blidah, and in three days I shall be in France."

It's ten o'clock, my friend. The bugle of the Turkish guard that I won't be hearing again is sounding the curfew. Good night. See you soon.

The Plain

Glossary

In the text the occasional definitions in parentheses following Arabic words are Fromentin's. His spelling has been followed with a few exceptions, such as Hawa not Haoûa, burnoose not *burnouss*.

amin   representative (as used here)

bab   gate, entry

balek!   watch out!

bey   high-ranking Ottoman official, provincial administrator

cadi   judge

caid   chief, judge

chachia   round brimless hat

chaouch   policeman, process server

crotals   ancient percussion instrument of Asian origin in wood, ivory, metal, or shell; castanets derive from them

darbouka   clay drum

dervish   member of various Muslim ascetic groups often noted for their devotional exercises

Dey   ruler of Algeria during the Turkish Regency (1671–1830)

diffa   repast, banquet

djebira   saddlebag

djerbi   woolen blanket

douar   encampment of tents, administrative division

douro   unit of currency, money; originally a Spanish coin

fhas   open country around a town, administered by it

foundouk   caravansary; when uppercased an agglomeration to the southeast of Algiers *fouta*   length of cloth wrapped around the waist

gandoura   sleeveless tunic worn under burnoose

haik   oblong cloth serving as outer garment

hautboy   ancestor of the oboe, whose name also derives from it

kasbah   fortress, citadel

khamsin   south wind off the desert, sirocco

kouba   dome atop tomb of a holy man or important person

marabout   1) religious leader, holy man; 2) tomb of such

mercanti   merchant in *sabir,* the local lingua franca

mizmoune   stringed instrument

mufti   high court judge, expert in religious law

oued   river, stream

razzia   raid

sarouel   pantaloons, Turkish trousers

sbed   1) perfume, musk 2) Saturday; by extension, market day

si, sid, sidi   male honorific, sir

smala   a chief's family and entourage including warriors; military
      encampment

spahi   a member of a cavalry group primarily made up of Algeri-
      ans, created by French in 1834

tell   cumulus, hill, fertile land

tolba   person who can read and write, a scribe

ya   polite interjection used when hailing someone

zouave   member of infantry group created by French in 1830

Notes

1. Hercules as one of his labors killed the winged, three-bodied monster, Geryon, scattering the torsos, which became Ibiza, Maiorca, and Menorca.

2. Syphax, king of western Numidia, died a captive in Rome in 200 BCE.

3. Hussein was the last Ottoman governor or Dey of Algeria.

4. The Fort of the Emperor was named for Charles V. The Spanish were finally expelled from Algiers in 1529.

5. Karel Dujardin and Nicholas Berchem are Dutch landscape painters whom Fromentin admired.

6. Mentioned ironically, this Bianca is the "Juliet" of François de Chateaubriand's tale of doomed love, *The Adventures of the Last of the Abencérages* (1826). A Moorish prince during the last days of Muslim rule in Granada, Aben-Hamed, the "Romeo," is in love with Blanca, a Christian girl who plays the guitar.

7. Abd-el-Kadr (1808–1883), an Algerian leader of recognized uprightness, will as well as intellectual and organizational ability, led resistance against the French for fifteen years. Finally surrendering in 1847, he was sent into exile.

8. In 1815 a British fleet under the command of Admiral Lord Exmouth, in retaliation for failure to release some Ionian slaves bombarded Algiers sinking the Dey's fleet, knocking out his shore batteries and causing much loss of life.

9. Fromentin again is reminded of Chateaubriand's novel, *The Adventures of the Last of the Abencérages* (see note 6). He likens this grave to that of the ill-starred Aben-Hamed. The two sentences Fromentin quotes conclude the novel. Chateaubriand, *Oeuvres romanesques et voyages,* vol. 2, p. 1401, Paris: Gallimard (Bibliothèque de la Pléiade) (1969).

10. Alexandre Decamps was the most popular French "Orientalist" painter of the romantic period.

11. Albano is the hero of German poet, satirist, and novelist Jean Paul Richter's four-volume novel, *Titan* (1800–1803).

12. Obermann is the protagonist of Etienne de Sénancourt's epistolary novel of the same name published in 1804. It had considerable influence on the romantic movement in Europe.

13. Sergeant Blandan and his outnumbered squad refused to surrender to Arab cavalry at Beni-Mered in 1842.

14. The Duke of Aumale, son of King Louis-Philippe and a career soldier, was governor of Constantine then briefly governor general of Algeria.

15. "Tomb of the Christian Woman" (Kouber-er-Roumiia) was the name given the burial cumulus of the Mauretanian kings. It relates specifically to the legend of a phantom woman from therein. This queen—her time would have been the late Roman Empire— once invoked the help of the spirit of Lake Haloula to stop thieves from plundering the graves' hoard of gold.

16. "The incantations make the acorns fall from the oak as well as the grapes from the vine" from Ovid's *Amores*, III, 7, 33–34.

17. The "unexpected and very important news" was the overthrow of the July Monarchy of Louis-Philippe, ushering in amid confusion the short-lived Second Republic.

18. That journal is *Un été au Sahara* (A summer in the Sahara), Fromentin's first book, published in 1857.

19. Fromentin quotes the French translation of William Shaler. The text presented here is from the American edition. Shaler, *Sketches of Algiers, Political, Historical, and Civil*, p. 222, Boston: Cummings, Hilliard, and Co. (1826).

20. The "'king' of the eighteenth century" undoubtedly means Voltaire.

21. "The greatest painter of the seventeenth century," means Nicholas Poussin, who spurned Louis XIV's Versailles for Rome.

22. "The monk of Fiesole" is Fra Angelico, born not far from there in Vicchio.

23. "One made a landscape out of the Orient; the second landscape and genre; while the third did genre and great painting," refers, in that order, to Prosper Marilhat (1811–1847); Alexandre Decamps (1803–1860); and Eugène Delacroix (1798–1863).

24. The landscape painter and Fromentin's teacher was Louis Cabat (1812–1893), who started out with the Barbizon open-air school but later worked in a more neoclassical style.

25. *The Masters of Past Time* (1876) on Dutch and Flemish art was Fromentin's last book. Victor Segalen, that remarkable writer and, *inter alia,* art historian, thought him nearly alone among "littérateurs" for writing cogently about painting: "meticulous, acute, invaluable criticism." "Gustave Moreau, Maître Imagier de l'Orphisme," essay of 1907 in Segalen, *Oeuvres complètes,* vol. 2, p. 703, Paris: Robert Lafont (1995).

26. An essay on the Salon of 1859 in Charles Baudelaire's *Curiosités Esthétiques* says of Fromentin, "He's strictly speaking neither landscape painter or painter of genre, those two fields being too restricted to contain his versatility and considerable fantasy." Baudelaire, *Oeuvres complètes,* p. 794, Paris: Gallimard (Bibliothèque de la Pléiade) (1951).

27. Thomas Shaw was an eighteenth-century British traveler. His *Travels, or Observations Relating to Several Parts of Barbary and the Levant* was still a standard reference for the region.

28. This was the old Algerian ensign, representing the three provinces and the Muslim faith.

29. "preceptor . . . and handsome of men" refers to the centaur Chiron and his pupil, Achilles.

30. In the 1850s "French Africa" meant, except for a couple of bases in Senegal, Algeria. The country at that time was called Algiers and included territory extending for at most one to two hundred miles into the interior.